THE

Rodgers
and
Hammerstein

STORY

THE

Rodgers
and
Hammerstein

STORY

Stanley Green

A DA CAPO PAPERBACK

Library of Congress Cataloging in Publication Data

Green, Stanley.
   The Rodgers and Hammerstein story.

   (A Da Capo Press paperback)
   Reprint of the ed. published by J. Day Co., New
York.
   Bibliography: p.
   Includes index.
   1. Rodgers, Richard, 1902-   2. Hammerstein,
Oscar, 1895-1960. I. Title.
[ML410.R6315G7 1980]   782.81′092′2 [B] 80-18339
ISBN 0-306-80124-8 (pbk.)

This Da Capo Press paperback edition of
The Rodgers and Hammerstein Story is an
unabridged republication of the first
edition published in New York in 1963 by
The John Day Company, supplemented with
new photographs and a revised Epilogue.
It is reprinted by arrangement with the author.

Published by Da Capo Press, Inc.
A Subsidiary of Plenum Publishing Corporation
227 West 17th Street, New York, N.Y. 10011

To Susan and Rudy,
who have been singing the songs
of Rodgers and Hammerstein almost
from the day they were born

Contents

CONTENTS

Illustrations will be found following page 126

Introduction

Rodgers and Hammerstein brought more of their own philosophies to the musical stage than any other American writers for that medium. Therefore, in writing this book about them, I have concentrated on their professional lives to bring out the personalities and character of the two.

The book is divided into two parts, the first devoted to their separate careers before their partnership and the second to their actual partnership. In the first part, I have written a parallel biography. That is, I have tried to show what both men were accomplishing at roughly the same time, indicating which features of their careers had the greatest influence on the development of the American musical theatre. Wherever possible, I have used direct quotations from Rodgers and Hammerstein. These have come mostly from newspapers, magazines, and the recorded conversations the men had with interviewer Arnold Michaelis. In the case of Mr. Rodgers, I have also benefited from personal conversations.

Since the book is mostly concerned with the outlooks and attitudes of Rodgers and Hammerstein as expressed through their musicals, I have purposely avoided quoting from critics' views on their productions. Critics' opinions are important, but very often they do not convey accurately the authors' intentions or the receptions given to the plays.

S.G.

Prologue

Oscar Hammerstein, 2nd, died on August 23, 1960, at the age of sixty-five. His death was not exactly unexpected. For well over a year, he had suffered from abdominal cancer, and his stocky frame had become gaunt and worn.

But death, no matter how well one may be prepared for it, never ceases to be a shock. Seldom before had so many people felt such a personal feeling of loss. So well were his plays and his songs known, that strangers even thought they somehow knew this shy, gentle man of the theatre. Next to Hammerstein's immediate family, of course, the person most affected by his death was Richard Rodgers, his partner of eighteen years. Rodgers and Hammerstein had become the most successful team in the entire history of the theatre, as well as the most influential. Their musical plays had a great effect on everything that had taken place in the musical theatre since *Oklahoma!*, their first collaboration in 1943. Now, with the deep realization that he would have to walk alone, Rodgers said simply, "I am permanently grieved."

To others who had worked with Oscar Hammerstein the shock was almost equally great. Mary Martin, then appearing in Rodgers and Hammerstein's last work, *The Sound of Music*, had to take a sedative before going on stage the night following Hammerstein's death. At the third and final curtain call after the play, she blew a heartfelt kiss to the balcony before collapsing backstage. The American Society of Composers, Authors and Publishers (ASCAP), the songwriters' performing rights organization, closed its offices for a day in tribute to a man who had been a member of its board of directors for 21 years. In a service preached two months after Hammerstein's death, Reverend Donald Harrington of the Community Church in New York acclaimed him as "one of the great spiritual leaders of our age." Perhaps playwright Howard Lindsay who, with Russel Crouse, was the author of *The Sound of Music*, summed up best the feeling of the entire theatrical profession when he wrote, "Those of us who work in the theatre always walked more proudly because Oscar Hammerstein was of the theatre."

The most unusual tribute took place about a week after Hammerstein's death. For three minutes, on the night of September 1st, the entire Times Square area in New York City was blacked out in honor of the man who had done so much to light up that particular part of the world. From 8:57 to 9:00 P.M., every neon sign and every light bulb was turned off and all traffic was halted between 42nd Street and 53rd Street, and between Eighth Avenue and the Avenue of the Americas. A crowd of 5,000, many with heads bowed, assembled at the base of the statue of Father Duffy on Times Square where two trumpeters blew taps. It was the most complete blackout on Broadway since World War II, and the greatest tribute of its kind ever paid to one man.

This and the other tributes were more than just expressions of respect to a talented man of the theatre. They were tributes to one who had brought so much of himself and his philosophy to a particular form of entertainment, and had helped to make the world a little friendlier because of it. In a sense, this outpouring of esteem and affection was not only for Oscar Hammerstein, but also for what Rodgers and Hammerstein stood for in the theatre. They had written nine musicals for the stage, one for the movies, and one for television, each one of them distinguished not alone for the way they said something but for what they said.

Even without personally knowing either man, it is possible to know a great deal about Rodgers and Hammerstein through their plays and songs. They revealed their authors to be, as novelist Herman Wouk once wrote, "not so much sophisticated as wise; not so much clever as civilized." They wrote with warmth, understanding, a decent outlook on life, a respect for their fellow man, a fondness for simple pleasures, and a basic feeling of optimism for the world. Their themes touched our heads as well as our hearts. Their plays did not preach sermons, but they did reveal their authors as two men who felt deeply about social problems. By never writing down to their audiences, Rodgers and Hammerstein helped to elevate them. By never following a proven hit formula, they paved the way for new talent to attempt daring and untrodden paths. Their influence was felt as strongly in front of the footlights as behind them.

As for the songs themselves, in each case the words fitted the music and the music fitted the words so perfectly that they seemed to be the product of one man. Yet, curiously, if the music of Rodgers can be enjoyed alone, so too can the lyrics of Hammerstein. Their songs have endured because they had something to say, both in their melodies and in their lyrics. They shed new insight on and new understanding of the eternal themes of love, fear, sadness, gaiety, hope, and so many others.

What was also important about the Rodgers and Hammerstein collaboration was their relationship to each other. They were men of similar outlooks on life. They came from similar middle-class backgrounds. They had similar habits: regular hours, no smoking, and only sociable drinking. They were influenced by the same currents that were shaping the form of the American musical theatre of the Twenties and the Thirties. They were both stagestruck all their lives. Most important, perhaps, they had probably the most harmonious partnership ever known in the theatre. And the consideration they showed each other was extended to everyone they had ever worked with. They had the respect of their co-workers because they always treated them with respect. They were proof that men of good will could succeed in a field all too frequently known for its jealousies and rivalries.

PART I

BACKGROUNDS

TO THE PARTNERSHIP

CHAPTER 1

Their Early Lives

It is surprising that Richard Rodgers and Oscar Hammerstein, who had known each other almost all of their lives, had to wait until Rodgers was forty and Hammerstein forty-seven before they could write together professionally. Although *Oklahoma!*, their first musical, helped set the pattern for the entire post World War II musical theatre, the works of each man before their partnership were of special importance. Through these works each man revealed the qualities that were to make Rodgers and Hammerstein such an ideal team.

Oscar Hammerstein was born into the theatre, but his parents wanted him to become a lawyer. Richard Rodgers' father was a doctor, but he encouraged his son to become a composer. Both men first lived in the general vicinity of Mount Morris Park, a small park in New York City at Fifth Avenue from 120th to 124th Streets. Hammerstein was born on July 12, 1895, on 135th Street, but his parents moved near the park when he was four. Rodgers was born June 28, 1902, at Ar-

[17

verne, Long Island, where his parents had a summer home. His home address was 3 West 120th Street.

At that time, the Mount Morris Park neighborhood consisted of well-kept brownstones and apartment houses. It was a highly desirable place for William and Alice Hammerstein to bring up their two sons, Oscar and Reginald. It was also a highly desirable place for William and Mamie Rodgers to bring up their two sons, Mortimer and Richard.

William Hammerstein was always called "Willie." He was the manager of one of the most successful vaudeville houses, the Victoria Theatre, which was owned by his father, who was also named Oscar Hammerstein. The first Oscar Hammerstein was a portly, bewhiskered gentleman who had emigrated from Germany during the Civil War. He became a cigar maker in New York, and he later invented a cigar-making machine that earned him a very large income. But because Oscar Hammerstein loved the theatre more than cigars, he soon managed to devote all his time to building theatres and producing shows. Of the ten theatres that he built in New York City, the most profitable was the Victoria, located at the corner of Seventh Avenue and 42nd Street. Today, the site is occupied by the Rialto Theatre. There, under Willie's smart management, many of the great vaudeville acts of the day performed.

Though most of his money came from vaudeville houses, Oscar Hammerstein's ambition was to be an opera impressario. For a while his Manhattan Opera House even rivaled the Metropolitan Opera House. This alarmed the Metropolitan's management so much that they gave Hammerstein one million dollars if he would stop producing operas in the United States for ten years. But that didn't stop Hammerstein. He used the million dollars to build the London Opera House. When this failed, he tried to produce opera again in New York. He was stopped only when the Metropolitan obtained a court order forbidding him.

One of Oscar Hammerstein's business habits was especially irritating to his son Willie. Whenever the elder Hammerstein needed money to pay his opera singers, he would simply go over to the Victoria Theatre box office and take most of the cash.

No wonder opera was a bad word in the home of Willie and Alice Hammerstein. In fact, they considered all show business a bad word. They were determined that no son of theirs would ever go into the theatre. It was far too risky, and all anyone ever got out of it were headaches and heartaches. Willie Hammerstein worked hard and kept late hours, and as a child Oscar saw very little of him. Whenever they did get together, Willie never spoke to his son about the tinseled world of two-a-day vaudeville that took up so much of his time.

Nevertheless, from time to time, Oscar could not help overhearing his parents talk about the theatre. It sounded like the mose exciting place in the world, and the boy begged to be taken to see it. At first his father said no. But after months of pleading, Willie Hammerstein agreed to take his four-year-old son to a matinee at the Victoria.

The big day arrived. Oscar, dressed in his best party suit, rode with his father on a series of trolley cars to get to the theatre. Once there, the boy sat alone in a box staring at the milling throng of people making their noisy way to their seats. Then, as the houselights dimmed and the audience quieted down, the orchestra struck up the music for the first act on the program and the curtain began to rise. Suddenly Oscar broke out in a cold sweat, his stomach fluttered, and his knees began to shake. He became so ill with excitement that he almost forgot where he was. This was a dream world and he was about to take his first look at heaven.

The act that opened that particular program at the Victoria was not really memorable. As Hammerstein recalled, it consisted of a group of young ladies drying a fishnet. Then one of them stepped away from the others and sang:

> Oh, I am a water maiden
> I live in the water
> A fisherman's daughter . . .

After a brief dance, the act was over. That's all there was to it. But to a stagestruck youth at his first show, this was Theatre. This was Glamour.

When his father took him backstage during the intermission, Oscar became so frightened by a caged lion from one of the acts on the bill that he felt sick to his stomach and begged to be taken home. There he was put right to bed. After sleeping soundly for fourteen hours, he announced to his mother that he now knew what he would do when he grew up. He had made up his mind that he too would go into the theatre.

In spite of this determination, young Oscar Hammerstein seldom had the opportunity of being with the famous grandfather after whom he was named. He was, however, very close to his maternal grandfather, James Nimmo. Grandfather Nimmo lived in an apartment just below the Hammersteins. For some unknown reason, Oscar slept in his grandparent's apartment, and had his meals with his mother and father.

Nimmo, who was a rather colorful character and resembled Mark Twain, had some unusual ideas of what to feed his grandson. At night, they would split a bottle of Guinness stout, and at six in the morning they had milk punch with whiskey. Though Hammerstein was no more than six at the time, this apparently never made him sick. It never made him a heavy drinker either, for Oscar rarely drank when he grew older.

After their morning drink, the old man and the boy would take a stroll to Mount Morris Park. There they would draw pictures, admire the flowers, and play games. They always walked up a hill near a bell tower. Every morning at seven a funny little man who was the bell ringer would climb the spiral staircase to the top of the tower to ring the bell announcing the time. This was the signal for grandfather and grandson to return home for their regular breakfast.

As a joke, Grandfather Nimmo always referred to the bell ringer as the Devil, and, of course, Oscar believed that he was. Since there was nothing frightening about the man, Oscar never feared the Devil. He found it hard to understand why anyone could possibly be afraid of a harmless little man who rang the bell every morning at seven in Mount Morris Park.

These walks and talks with his grandfather had a great influence on the young boy. Although Oscar may have inherited his love for the theatre from Grandfather Hammerstein, it was Grandfather Nimmo who helped to shape his healthy, optimistic view of life.

Richard Rodgers first became aware of the world of the theatre at an even earlier age than did Oscar Hammerstein. He was two years old when he first began to hear his mother and father singing the songs from the latest musical comedies and operettas. In those days, people took home the complete vocal scores from the leading Broadway attractions, just as today people buy original-cast long-playing records. With the music propped up on the family piano, Mrs. Rodgers would accompany her own singing of the female parts, while Dr. Rodgers, who had a fine baritone, would sing the male parts. "Anything that happens to you at the age of two," Rodgers later said, "especially if it has emotional and intellectual impact, is bound to influence you."

These family concerts took place for many years, and it wasn't long before Dick had memorized the words to all the songs. At four, he was trying to find the right notes on the piano to fit the songs. By the time he was six, he had taught himself to play with both hands.

Rodgers' devotion to music from an early age delighted both his parents. They made sure that he took piano lessons, and when he showed talent in composing, they encouraged him to make his career in music. This attitude on the part of Rodgers' parents was extremely unusual. Most parents who learn that their child is anxious to pursue a musical career do everything to stop him. The musical theatre is crowded with composers and lyricists who succeeded despite the opposition of well-meaning fathers, such as Oscar Hammerstein's, who sincerely felt that show business was a far too risky way of earning a living.

But Dr. Rodgers' faith in his son's ability never wavered. Although he was not rich, he did have a good practice. It allowed him to give his son financial as well as moral support, and Dick was always grateful. The fact that he never knew hunger, Rodgers believes, was what helped him keep his head and not spend his money foolishly when he did win success as a composer. And the encouragement and understanding of his mother and father may well have given him an added desire to succeed in order to justify their faith.

Oscar Hammerstein, of course, could not spend all of his time at vaudeville shows—much as he would have loved to. His parents moved downtown to 91st Street and Central Park West when he was seven. For a while he attended Public School 9, at 82nd Street and West End Avenue. At nine, he was sent to Hamilton Institute, a semimilitary school. It was there that he wrote his first story, "The Adventures of a Penny," which was published in the school newspaper.

When he was twelve, Oscar spent his first summer at Weingart's Institute, a summer camp at Highmount, N.Y. The camp was organized so that the mornings were devoted to studies and the afternoons to sports. Young Oscar—or "Oc" as he was called—was particularly fond of tennis and baseball, and was a fairly good athlete.

More than anything, however, Oscar Hammerstein enjoyed the simple pleasures of living in the country for the two months of the camp season. He would take long walks through the neighboring countryside, just smelling the grass and admiring the view. The sight of mountains and forests and lakes filled him with a never-ending love for the wonders of nature. This love was to deepen and to find expression in some of his most memorable lyrics.

At Weingart's, Hammerstein made many of the friends he was to keep all his life. Lorenz Hart, later to become Rodgers' first song-writing partner, was there for at least one season. Others with whom Hammerstein formed lasting friendships were Leighton K. Brill and Sig Herzig. Brill became Hammerstein's assistant in 1926 and was with him for almost thirty years; Herzig later won fame as a Hollywood writer and co-author of the musical, *Bloomer Girl*.

Rodgers, like Hammerstein, also started going to the theatre at an early age. When he was six, his parents took him to see DeWolf Hopper in *The Pied Piper* during its run at a local theatre on 125th Street. Shortly after that, Dick went to see his first musical at a regular Broadway theatre. This was Victor Herbert's *Little Nemo*, a fitting choice for a boy because it was based on a popular comic strip. The theatre that it played in was the New Amsterdam, located about a half block from Hammerstein's Victoria.

From then on, Rodgers was a steady theatregoer. Sometimes his parents would take him to see shows on Broadway. At other times he would see them at the neighborhood theatres where the musicals toured after their Broadway engagements.

Rodgers cannot remember a time when he did not want to be a composer for the theatre. "Before I began writing I was a baby," he once told a television interviewer. Everything that went into the making of a musical fascinated the serious-minded youth. He would see his favorites over and over again just to study how they were put together.

Of course, it was the music that interested him most. It wasn't long before he was able to make up his own tunes at the piano. And not long after that, he was able to write the notes down on paper.

Oscar Hammerstein was fifteen when his mother died. Although she had been in frail health during most of her life, this was a great shock to the boy. He did everything he could to keep from breaking down. He bought a large picture album and pasted pictures in it of his sports heroes. He took long, lonely walks trying to think things through. He never went to his father or anyone else. He knew that he would have to adjust to the situation by himself. This strength of character was to be with him all through his life. He always felt that grief should be resisted because it was an enemy that had to be beaten.

Hammerstein was then living at 87th Street and Central Park West. About the same time, the Rodgers family also decided to move downtown from the Mount Morris Park area. Their new address was 161 West 86th Street, just about two blocks away from the Hammersteins. Since a sixteen-year-old young man would have little in common with a nine-year-old boy, it was not surprising that Oscar and Dick never met. And besides, Rodgers was devoting his time—while he wasn't at Public School 166—to his piano lessons.

In 1912, at the age of seventeen, Oscar Hammerstein entered Columbia University. This was time for a serious talk between father and son. Willie Hammerstein made Oscar promise that he would never do anything as stupid as making the theatre his lifework. His son obediently agreed. It never occurred to him to do anything else but obey his father's wishes. His father wanted him to become a lawyer, and that was what he was going to be.

Oscar got good grades in college. He also played first base on the freshman baseball team during the spring, though he was never able to make the varsity. He even tried out for the football team, but he was too light. The extracurricular activity that interested him most, however, was the Varsity Show. The Varsity Show was the over-all name given to an annual musical satire usually written by undergraduates. All the parts were played by students and, because Columbia was an all-male college, this meant that some of them would have to be dressed as women. The shows usually had professional assistance, including professional musicians in the orchestra. They were always presented for a week in March at the Astor Hotel Grand Ballroom.

Oscar's first Varsity Show was called *On Your Way*. It was produced in 1915, and his part was that of a comic poet. The death of Hammerstein's father earlier in the school year somehow had freed Oscar from his pledge not to go near the theatre. Besides, this was only an amateur show.

Mortimer Rodgers, Dick's older brother, also went to Columbia at that time, and was a member of the same fraternity that Hammerstein belonged to. Well aware of his brother's passion for the theatre, Mortimer took Dick to see a Saturday matinee performance of *On Your Way*. After the show, while the ballroom was being cleared for dancing, Richard Rodgers, aged twelve, met Oscar Hammerstein, aged nineteen, for the first time.

The meeting under such circumstances was certainly not one between two equals. Rodgers was completely in awe of the worldly college junior who had had the leading comic role in the most important theatrical event of the school season. For his part, Hammerstein tried his best to impress the stagestruck youth with his mature charm. Years later, in recalling this meeting, Rodgers stoutly maintained that he was wearing long pants at the time. Hammerstein, however, insisted that he was wearing short pants. This difference of opinion was the only "argument" that the partners ever had during the more than 18 years that they worked together.

Oscar secretly loved acting and writing more than anything else, and even then his literary talents were being noticed. One afternoon, as his junior year was almost over, he had a talk with Professor Carl Van Doren about his future. When Oscar told the distinguished teacher that he was going to law school, the professor looked surprised. Oscar asked him what was wrong. "Oh, nothing," Van Doren replied, "except that I thought you should write."

Van Doren had guessed Hammerstein's secret. "This guess was a kind of endorsement of a wild dream," Hammerstein later said. "I left his office and floated down Morningside Drive filled with an ambition that now seemed more possible than I had ever believed it to be."

In spite of his pride at hearing such encouragement, Hammerstein still felt that he should follow his father's wishes and become a lawyer. He entered Columbia Law School in the fall of 1915 (this would have been his senior year), but he still would not give up acting and writing. In the spring, he again took part in the Varsity Show, this time writing a special scene in it for himself. The show, a parody on Henry Ford's peace expedition during World War I, was called *The Peace Pirates*.

Dick Rodgers, like Hammerstein, had been sent by his parents to Weingart's Institute, in the summer of 1914. Two years later, when he was fourteen, Rodgers went to Camp

Wigwam, near Harrison, Maine. Apart from swimming, he cared little for sports. Music was almost his only love, and he could usually be found at the piano entertaining his fellow campers. Encouraged by the music counselor, Robert Lippmann, Dick wrote the words and music for a camp song, "Dear Old Wigwam," and the melody for another, "Camp-Fire Days."

After dropping out of Townsend Harris High School the previous term, Rodgers entered DeWitt Clinton High School in the fall of 1916. That was the year he became interested in opera after seeing a performance of *Carmen* at the Metropolitan Opera House. It was also the year he discovered his musical idol.

Unlike Hammerstein, Rodgers never had the problem of choosing a career. He wanted to become a composer, his parents wanted him to become a composer, and that was that. He knew too that he wanted to compose for the theatre, but it was not until he saw the early musicals of Jerome Kern that he knew exactly what kind of musical theatre he wanted to write for.

Kern had been composing songs for operettas and musical comedies almost since the turn of the century. Then in 1915, he became part of a new movement in musical comedy. That movement centered around the intimate musicals then being introduced at the tiny Princess Theatre. Kern wrote most of his scores in collaboration with Guy Bolton and P. G. Wodehouse. What made the Princess Theatre musicals different was that they told logical stories in modern settings with believable characters caught in everyday situations. Most important, the songs were used as part of the action of these stories.

Today, such productions would not seem unusual. But in the mid-1910s, Broadway was overrun by English versions of European operettas. Though their music was often lovely, they all seemed to be about princes in disguise and starry-eyed peasant maidens. They were usually located in mythical king-doms, and were far from the experiences and emotions of American audiences.

Bolton, Wodehouse and Kern led the rebellion against this form of the unreal, overstuffed musical. And one of their most ardent followers was a fourteen-year-old boy named Richard Rodgers.

Almost every Saturday afternoon, young Rodgers would climb the stairs to the balcony of a theatre where a Jerome Kern musical would be playing. Some of them he would see on Broadway; others at local theatres where the shows would be presented after their Broadway run. He saw *Very Good Eddie* at least a dozen times at the Standard Theatre on 90th and Broadway. And he was almost equally loyal to other Kern musicals such as *Oh, Boy!*, *Love o' Mike*, *Leave It to Jane*, and *Oh, Lady! Lady!!* "If you were at all sensitive to music," Rodgers later said, "Kern had to be your idol. You had to worship Kern."

While Rodgers was attending DeWitt Clinton High School, Hammerstein was doggedly trying to concentrate on his law studies. It was his second year at law school, but the bright spot on the calendar was still the Varsity Show. This one was called *Home, James*. Hammerstein wrote the book and lyrics with another student, Herman Axelrod, and the music was composed by the same Robert Lippmann who had urged Dick Rodgers to write songs at Camp Wigwam. Oscar again played the leading comic role. He made such a hit as a French head-waiter that a club in Brooklyn paid him $8 for a one-night appearance doing a routine from the show with two other students.

Hammerstein's income at the time was $50 a week from securities left by his father. That may have been all right for a twenty-one-year-old law school student without responsibilities. But Oscar wanted to get married and he needed more money to support a wife. The girl he had chosen was a distant relative of Dick Rodgers named Myra Finn, whom he had met one summer at Highmount, New York.

In order to earn extra money and to gain experience in the legal field, Hammerstein took a part-time job with the law firm of Blumenstiel and Blumenstiel. All he was paid, however, was $5 a week.

Oscar was now desperate. He felt that his combined income of $55 a week was still not enough money to get married on. Therefore, he took the only other course open to him. Despite his promise to his father, Oscar asked his uncle, Arthur Hammerstein, for a job. Arthur Hammerstein was then one of the most successful producers on Broadway. He had been the general manager of *Naughty Marietta*, which his father, the original Oscar Hammerstein, had produced in 1910. Since then, he had gone on his own to produce such hits as *The Firefly*, *High Jinks*, and *Katinka*, all with music by Rudolf Friml and lyrics and libretto by Otto Harbach.

Arthur was sympathetic to his nephew's desire to go into the theatre, and he agreed to give him the job on the condition that Oscar would not write anything for a year. He would have to learn about the theatre from the bottom up. This meant that he would work as an office boy and read plays during the day, and work as assistant stage manager at night. In this way, Oscar would become familiar with every step in the creation of a play—writing, directing, acting, designing, and producing. If he were serious, he could learn all there was to know about the theatre. The salary was $20 a week.

Not only did this job pay $15 more per week than he was earning at the law office, it would be an opportunity to prepare for the kind of work he really loved. He promptly accepted the offer, quit law school, and went to work on *You're In Love*, another Friml-Harbach musical that had been running since February. That summer—1917—Oscar married Myra Finn.

At a time when Oscar Hammerstein was being prevented from writing, Richard Rodgers was receiving every encouragement. In June, 1917, he took out his first musical copyright. It was for the song "Auto Show Girl," with lyrics by a friend named David Dyrenforth. Rodgers had the song multigraphed and distributed among his family and friends. He was also writing other songs with lyrics by his brother Mortimer or by his father.

Mortimer was responsible for getting Dick his first assignment to write a musical comedy score. Mortimer was a member of a social group called the Akron Club. Soon after the United States had entered World War I, the club planned to put on a musical show as a benefit for the New York *Sun*'s Tobacco Fund for servicemen. To Mortimer, this was a great opportunity for his brother. In spite of opposition to hiring such a young composer, the fifteen-year-old boy was selected to write the score. Aided by his family, Rodgers turned out seven songs for the production, which was called *One Minute, Please*. The show was presented at the Plaza Hotel Grand Ballroom on December 29, 1917, and, thanks to the generosity of Dr. Rodgers, Dick was able to publish some of the songs and to have them sold in the lobby. Among the titles were "When They Rub Noses In Alaska," "I'm a Vampire," and "At the Movies" ("If your sweetie should prove fickle, You can love her for a nickel").

Although Oscar Hammerstein was faithful to his promise not to write anything for a year as far as the professional theatre was concerned, he just could not resist doing another Varsity Show, even though he no longer attended Columbia. Thus, in the spring of 1918, the "War Show," *Ten for Five*, was presented with book and lyrics by Oscar Hammerstein and music by Robert Lippmann. While he did not appear in this production, Hammerstein kept himself busy by directing the show.

CHAPTER 2

Rodgers Meets Hart,
Hammerstein Meets Stothart

In 1919, Richard Rodgers was writing songs with many different people. One thing, however, was clear: he needed a regular lyric-writing partner. Philip Leavitt, a classmate of Mortimer's at Columbia, had an idea. He knew a lyric writer who needed a composer. Why not introduce Dick to him?

Phil Leavitt's lyric-writing friend was Lorenz Hart. Hart, who was a descendant of Heinrich Heine, the German poet, was born in New York on May 2, 1895. He had first lived on 111th Street near Lexington Avenue, but his family moved to 119th Street when he was nine. This was a block away from Rodgers' former home. Hart went to Weingart's Institute (both the school in New York City and the camp at Highmount), Columbia Grammar School, and Columbia University. He saw his first play when he was seven, and he was devoted to the plays of Shakespeare even at an early age.

Leavitt arranged to have Rodgers meet Hart on a Sunday afternoon. Phil and Dick traveled to 119th Street by subway, climbed the front stoop of Hart's brownstone house, and were greeted by Larry at the door. Hart, who never grew more than five feet, had a very swarthy complexion which was made all the more swarthy that morning because he needed a shave. He wore a pair of tuxedo trousers, an undershirt, and a pair of house slippers. In spite of his odd appearance, however, he was a middle-aged man of the world to the naïve sixteen-year-old Rodgers. Hart, in fact, was part of the professional theatre at that time since he earned his living by translating German plays for the Shubert brothers, the famous producers.

Rodgers was fascinated by everything that Hart had to say. He learned about different kinds of rhymes, and the wide range of subjects that could be dealt with in a popular song. He learned about the purpose of lyrics in a play, and how they should say something about the characters and the story. He was especially delighted that Hart was also a great admirer of the Bolton, Wodehouse and Kern musicals that had been presented at the Princess Theatre. This was the kind of musical theatre that both Rodgers and Hart wanted to be a part of.

At their first meeting, Hart was as impressed by Rodgers' music as Rodgers was by Hart's lyrics and ideas. Nothing was said about a partnership. The two young men simply had a feeling that they could write together. "I left Hart's house," Rodgers wrote half-jokingly twenty years later, "having acquired in one afternoon a career, a partner, a best friend, and a source of permanent irritation."

At the time that Dick and Larry began experimenting with music and lyrics, Oscar Hammerstein was taking advantage of the opportunity to learn every aspect of the professional theatre. In the fall of 1918, he had graduated from assistant stage manager to full stage manager for *Sometime*, which starred Ed Wynn. The following March, he had the same job for *Tumble In,* a show that was described in its program as "a comic rhapsody in two raps and four taps." The dependable Rudolf Friml was the composer for both, and Otto Harbach was the librettist-lyricist for *Tumble In.*

Now, at last, Oscar felt that he was ready to write his first professional play. He had worked for his uncle for more than a year without trying to write anything of his own. By carefully watching and listening, he had picked up many worthwhile ideas about writing for the theatre, and he was confident that he could put this experience to use. For his debut as a playwright, Hammerstein wrote a drama without music called *The Light.* Yet in spite of his training, it was obvious that he still had a lot to learn. The play was very amateurish and lasted only four performances in New Haven.

Hammerstein was naturally disappointed, but it did make him realize that perhaps he might be better suited to writing musicals than to writing dramas. He discussed the matter with Herbert Stothart, who was the musical director of most of Uncle Arthur's productions. Stothart liked the idea of teaming up with Hammerstein to write a full musical comedy score, and they lost no time in getting to work.

Since Rodgers and Hart were then only concerned with writing songs and did not have the problem of dreaming up stories to go with them, they had their first professional work on Broadway before Stothart and Hammerstein did. This was the song "Any Old Place with You."

Again it was Phil Leavitt who helped them out. Since he had been the one who brought them together, he felt that he should do what he could to help Rodgers and Hart sell their songs. In the summer of 1919, Leavitt's family had a summer home in Far Rockaway near the home of Lew Fields. Fields had been a favorite German dialect comedian with his partner

Joe Weber in the latter part of the 1800s. They had split up in 1912, and both were now producing and acting in their own separate shows. Leavitt made an appointment for Rodgers and Hart to audition their songs for Fields in his home. There the team met not only the famous actor, but also two of his children; Dorothy, who later became a famous lyricist herself, and Herbert, who was to supply the books of many of the early Rodgers and Hart musicals.

Of all the songs that Rodgers played for him that summer afternoon, Lew Fields was most impressed with "Any Old Place with You." He promptly decided to add it to the score of his current musical, *A Lonely Romeo*, which was then running in New York. This practice of just taking a catchy song and inserting it in a show already on Broadway is almost unheard of today. However, as Rodgers recalls, "In those days, all a show tune needed to be acceptable was attractiveness and a potential hit quality." The remarkable thing about "Any Old Place with You" was that one-half of the team that gave it these qualities was a seventeen-year-old boy just out of high school.

That summer and fall, the other new team, Stothart and Hammerstein, worked busily on their show. Oscar may not have known how to write a straight nonmusical play, but he was certain that he knew all about writing a musical. After all, he had been going to see musical shows since he was four, he had written two Varsity Shows, and he had already had a two-year professional apprenticeship.

Hammerstein confidently believed that all that was needed for a musical to succeed were funny jokes, love songs, fast dancing, and some pretty girls in the chorus. He was sure that the last thing audiences cared about was a good story. Therefore, in preparing for his Broadway debut as a librettist and lyricist, he paid more attention to writing funny lines for the comedians and clever words for the songs than he did to the development of the characters and plot.

When his show first opened its tryout tour in Providence, Rhode Island, Hammerstein was surprised at the lack of reaction to what he thought were the funniest lines in the show. Then he got a really big shock when he heard the audience laugh at a line that wasn't supposed to be funny. He couldn't understand it until he realized that it got such a laugh because it referred to a funny line in a previous scene. To his amazement, he discovered that the audience had been paying careful attention to the story. That gave him the first inkling of the importance of the plot in a musical comedy.

The musical that marked the Broadway debut of Oscar Hammerstein and Herbert Stothart was first called *Joan of Arkansaw*, then *Toinette*, and finally, when it reached New York, *Always You*. That was in January, 1920. Although Hammerstein had begun to realize his mistakes during the tryout, he was unable to correct them in time. As a result, he showed far greater promise as a lyric writer than as a book writer. Arthur Hammerstein, who produced *Always You*, thought that his nephew needed a more experienced partner, someone who could teach him the techniques of putting together the very complicated form of entertainment known as musical comedy.

Therefore, Arthur suggested that Oscar join with Otto Harbach in writing both the book and the lyrics. Both men were pleased with the idea: Oscar because he could learn so much from the older man, and Otto Harbach because he welcomed the chance to guide a young man of such obvious talent.

Teaching came naturally to the kindly Harbach, who was twenty-two years older than Hammerstein. Born in Salt Lake City in 1873, he had been a professor of English at Whitman College in Walla Walla, Washington, before becoming a

newspaper reporter in New York. His first love, however, was
the theatre. In 1908, his initial show, *The Three Twins*, became a hit, and so did one of his songs in it, "Cuddle Up a
Little Closer, Lovey Mine." *Madame Sherry*, two years later,
was an even bigger success, and it had an equally popular song,
"Every Little Movement Has a Meaning All Its Own." Both
of these scores had music by Karl Hoschna. In 1912, Harbach
formed a partnership with composer Rudolf Friml to write
The Firefly. This became one of Harbach's most beloved
musicals, and began his association with producer Arthur
Hammerstein.

While working on a new musical with Harbach and Stothart, Oscar Hammerstein still found time to serve as one of
three judges to pick the Columbia University Varsity Show
of 1920. To no one's surprise, Dick Rodgers had entered Columbia the previous fall, and also to no one's surprise, his main
reason for choosing Columbia was the chance to write a Varsity Show. He and Larry Hart lost no time in writing a show
which they then submitted to the judges. Hammerstein and
the other two members of the panel liked the songs, but they
suggested to Hart that he might have a stronger story if he
would base his libretto on a play called *Fly With Me*, which
had been submitted by another alumnus named Milton
Kroopf. Hart agreed, and rewrote Kroopf's story with the
assistance of Phil Leavitt. Their final product, a musical satire
of undergraduate life on an island ruled by the Soviets, was
then approved enthusiastically by the committee. The show
was presented at the Astor Hotel Ballroom on March 24,
1920, with Rodgers conducting the 24-piece orchestra.

The score of *Fly With Me* contained 13 songs, 12 written
by Rodgers and Hart, and one written by Rodgers and Hammerstein. The circumstances surrounding the creation of that
number, "Room for One More," have long been forgotten and

so has the song. But the lyric, perhaps suggesting Oscar's fondness for the poetry of John Donne, is worth noting:

> My heart is an airy castle
>   Filled with girls I adore.
> My brain is a cloud of memories
>   Of peaches galore.
> There were Jane and Molly,
>   And Ruth and Sue;
> Camilla, Kit and Patricia, too.
> My heart is filled to the brim with you—
> But there's always room for one more!

This was to be the only collaboration between Rodgers and Hammerstein for 23 years.

CHAPTER *3*

The Successful Twenties

Fly With Me was well received, but Rogers and Hart were hardly prepared for the good fortune it promised to bring them so quickly. Soon after the show opened, Lew Fields, who had seen one of the performances, announced that he would use most of the songs in the score of his new musical, *Poor Little Ritz Girl*. Here was an almost unbelievable opportunity for the seventeen-year-old college freshman and his twenty-four-year-old partner. Hart promptly set about changing lyrics to fit the new show in addition to writing new songs with Rodgers.

By the time *Poor Little Ritz Girl* opened in Boston in May, 1920, only three songs from *Fly With Me* were included in the 15 numbers that made up the score. "Don't Love Me Like Othello" became "You Can't Fool Your Dreams"; the Oriental-flavored "Peek In Pekin" became "Love's Intense In Tents"; and "Dreaming True" became "Love Will Call." At least two of the other songs had been heard previously in another amateur musical, *You'd Be Surprised*.

But no matter what the origins of the songs were, the important thing to Rodgers and Hart was that they would soon have a complete Broadway score to their credit. This, unfortunately, did not turn out to be the case. During the Boston run of *Poor Little Ritz Girl*, Lew Fields began to have doubts about entrusting such an important assignment to two inexperienced young men. Therefore, he made a decision: he would get rid of about half the songs and substitute the same number by the better-known team of Sigmund Romberg and Alex Gerber.

Having sold their songs outright to Fields, Rodgers and Hart had no idea of what was going on until they showed up at the opening night performance in New York. It was only then that they discovered to their dismay that half of their songs had been thrown out. Their only consolation was that perhaps half a score was better than none, and they hoped that at least some of their work would be noticed.

Within a month after the opening of *Poor Little Ritz Girl*, Oscar Hammerstein had his first Broadway hit. It was called *Tickle Me*, and it had a libretto by Hammerstein, Harbach and Frank Mandel, lyrics by Hammerstein and Harbach, and music by Stothart. The success was only partly due to the literary and musical qualities of the show, since it starred Frank Tinney, one of the most popular entertainers in vaudeville. *Tickle Me* had an impressive run for its day of 207 Broadway performances, and then toured for seven months.

Possibly because *Poor Little Ritz Girl* had had only a fair run, and possibly because producers thought Rodgers and Hart were too young, the team could find no one willing to take another chance on them. For Dick Rodgers there was nothing else to do but go back to Columbia—and write the Varsity Show of 1921, *You'll Never Know*. Neither Lew Fields nor anyone else was interested in the songs. The show did, however, reunite Rodgers with Hammerstein because Oscar was one of three alumni who directed it. Lew Fields' son, Herbert, staged the dances, and Rodgers again conducted the orchestra.

Having had their hopes built up and then dashed so quickly was extremely disheartening to Rodgers and Hart. This, however, did not cause Dick to change his mind about a career. In fact, he now was so determined to succeed as a composer that he quit Columbia after his sophomore year to enroll in the Institute of Musical Art (now known as the Juilliard School of Music).

Rodgers spent two years at the Institute, studying harmony and ear training, and attending lectures in musical history. While still a student he was permitted a leave of absence to conduct a touring vaudeville unit. Upon finishing his studies, Rodgers joined Hart in writing amateur shows for any school or club or religious group that asked them. Although they were kept busy, they earned very little money. And, what was most painful, no one had enough faith in them to ask them to write a Broadway score.

During these years in the early Twenties, Hammerstein was not doing especially well, either. He had four failures in a row after *Tickle Me*. Then, early in February, 1923, he found himself almost unexpectedly with one of the biggest hits of the Twenties. The musical was *Wildflower*, for which Hammerstein and Harbach did the libretto and lyrics, and Herbert Stothart and Vincent Youmans did the music. Youmans was only twenty-five at the time, but had already shown his great gift for creating strikingly original melodies.

Although *Wildflower* caught on and ran for over a year on

Broadway, its story was rather simple-minded. What distinguished it was a general gaiety, some fine singing, and some lovely Vincent Youmans music. In its Italian setting and in its choruses of smiling peasant maidens, there was also a touch of operetta about the production. But there was a decidedly up-to-date quality in the way the songs fitted the action of the plot.

The following year, 1924, both Hammerstein and Rodgers tried their luck at writing plays without music. Hammerstein's two works, *Gypsy Jim* and *New Toys*, were written with Milton Herbert Gropper. Both plays were failures. Rodgers and Hart, with Herbert Fields as co-author, wrote a comedy for Lew Fields, but it fared just as badly. The title of the play was *The Melody Man*, and the shy trio used the pen name "Herbert Richard Lorenz." Though the show was not a musical, two satirical songs, "I'd Like to Poison Ivy" and "Moonlight Mama," were sung in it.

At a time when Rodgers and Hart were tasting nothing but failure, Hammerstein became associated with an even bigger hit than *Wildflower*. *Rose-Marie* was another four-man collaboration, this time involving Hammerstein, Harbach, Stothart, and Harbach's longtime partner, composer Rudolf Friml.

In many ways, *Rose-Marie* was a very daring musical. Hammerstein actually thought of it as the beginning of a new age in the musical theatre. It was something of a follow-up to *Wildflower* in its foreign setting, its dependence on well-trained singers, and its attempt at integration of songs to story.

The word "integration" requires some added comment. Certainly, musical plays were never created as a form of realistic entertainment. It is completely unnatural for two people to burst into song in the middle of a conversation, or for a row of men and women to sing in unison and then go into a complicated dance step. How to make these unreal things believable to an audience requires a combination of many skills. What is required most of all is that the musical portions of a show blend smoothly with the story so that they should never seem forced or awkward. Songs can be blended in three major ways: they can help to set the right mood; they can reveal character; and they can advance the story. Sometimes a song can do all three, but if it accomplishes just one of these functions, it is usually considered to be integrated. Except for the Bolton, Wodehouse and Kern shows, little attention was paid to integration in the first two decades of this century. The fact that Rodgers and Hart's "Any Old Place With You" was added to the score of a show then running on Broadway is an example of this lack of concern.

Making the songs fit into the story was taken very seriously by the writers of *Rose-Marie*. They even put the following note in the theatre program:

> The musical numbers of this play are such an integral part of the action that we do not think we should list them as separate episodes. The songs which stand out, independent of their dramatic association, are "Rose-Marie," "Indian Love Call," "Totem Tom-Tom," and "Why Shouldn't We?" in the first act, and "The Door of Her Dreams" in the second act.

When seen in a revival today, *Rose-Marie* might not appear to be a very good example of musical integration. Many of its attempts at fitting the songs into the story were awkwardly done. The important thing, however, is that it was a pioneering effort in the creation of a more mature musical theatre.

It was also a very real expression of Hammerstein's views on the musical theatre. He had seen the great wave of European-type operettas give way to the fast-moving, up-to-date musical farces of the Twenties. Although he admired many of these modern shows, he did not feel that type of musical entertainment would last. He was convinced that the most durable form of musical show was the one that depended more on good singing voices than on clever footwork. And in order to show off these voices to their best effect, he felt that stronger, more realistic stories were needed. The plot of *Rose-Marie* was actually concerned with a murder, and the way the guilty party was eventually caught. This was an almost revolutionary theme for a light musical production.

Hammerstein also believed that the successes of *Wildflower* and particularly of *Rose-Marie* would lead the way toward a form of light opera that would seriously challenge grand opera. He saw the musical stage becoming more dramatic in subject matter and more operatic in musical quality. Furthermore, he felt that the believable stories and characters of such works would give them a wide appeal. He was, of course, a bit ahead of his time. *Rose-Marie* started no such movement. But Hammerstein's later works with Jerome Kern and Richard Rodgers clearly lived up to the kind of musical theater that he could only dream about in 1924.

Oscar Hammerstein at twenty-nine had reached the Broadway heights in four and a half years. Richard Rodgers at twenty-two was plunged into almost total despair. Nothing seemed to be working out. The bright promise that he had shown ever since he was sixteen was not being fulfilled—at least not on Broadway. He felt that he could no longer spend his time on amateur shows just to gain experience. He would have to make a decision soon about what path he should follow. This decision was made even more difficult in a way because his father never once said anything to him about going out and finding a job. Dr. Rodgers was willing to continue to support his son, and to encourage him in his musical career. But Dick's conscience was bothering him. He felt that perhaps the time had come for him to settle down to something more profitable than writing songs.

Through a friend, he met a manufacturer of children's underwear. The man needed a new salesman whom he hoped to train to take over the business after he retired. He was impressed with Rodgers and offered him the position at a salary of $50 a week. This would be a good job at a good salary, and Rodgers was flattered at the man's faith in him. But he still wanted a little time to think things over.

Rodgers spent a restless night going over the whole proposal, and by morning he had almost talked himself into accepting the offer. That very morning he received a telephone call. It was from a friend, Ben Kaye, a lawyer and occasional lyric writer, who wanted to know if Rodgers would be interested in writing a score for a new revue. It would not be just another amateur show. The cast would be made up of young actors and actresses then appearing in bit parts in Theatre Guild productions, and they planned their revue to serve a double purpose. It would give a lot of talented young people a chance to be noticed by Broadway audiences. It would also benefit the Theatre Guild by helping to pay for some badly needed tapestries at its new theatre on 52nd Street.

It did not take much persuading to convince Rodgers. This was what he had been waiting for: a fresh, intimate, satirical revue that would provide just the right setting for his songs. He expressed his regrets to the children's wear manufacturer, and went back to his real business of writing songs.

Rodgers, of course, insisted that Larry Hart be signed to write the lyrics. In addition to their new material, they used a song they had written a few years before for an unproduced musical called *Winkle Town*. Nothing had ever happened with that show—even after Hammerstein had been called in to lend a hand at revising the book—and Rodgers and Hart did not want to see one of its songs go to waste. The song was "Manhattan," and when Lawrence Langner and Theresa Helburn, the directors of the Theatre Guild, heard it and the other numbers, they promised to sponsor the new revue. The Garrick Theatre, in which it was to be housed, supplied them with the title for the show: *The Garrick Gaieties.*

No one had any idea what to expect of this entertainment when it gave its first of two scheduled performances on May 17, 1925. But the wit of the sketches, the enthusiasm of the talented cast, and the charm and originality of the songs made it an overnight hit. Early in June, *The Garrick Gaieties* began a series of regular performances and the run lasted through November.

The Garrick Gaieties made everyone concerned very happy. Such talented actors as Sterling Holloway, Libby Holman, Romney Brent, and Philip Loeb (who directed the show) soon graduated to important parts in the theatre and movies. The Theatre Guild got its tapestries and some extra money besides. And Rodgers and Hart swiftly became the most talked-about young songwriters in the theatre.

Years later, at a fashionable opening night at the Guild Theatre, Larry Hart nudged his partner. "See those tapestries, Dick," he said. "We're responsible for them." "No, Larry," Rodgers replied, "You've got it backwards. *They're* responsible for *us.*"

There was no question about it. *The Garrick Gaieties* was not a false start as *Poor Little Ritz Girl* had been. However, this did not mean that every producer's office would now be open to Rodgers and Hart.

They tried to follow up their success by offering producers a musical they had written the previous year called *Dear Enemy.* Because Herbert Fields had created the book, it seemed only natural that they should first show it to his father. But Lew Fields said no. The show would never succeed, he told them. It was about an incident in the American Revolution, and everyone knew that a successful musical could not be made out of a page of American history. If it were set in some mythical country, that would be all right. Or a modern tale about the problems of Prohibition among Long Island society people would also have a chance. But never anything that had to do with such a serious subject as America's struggle for independence.

Other producers also turned down the show. Rodgers and Hart finally managed to interest a popular musical comedy star, Helen Ford, and she, in turn, managed to get her husband to produce it. With the title changed to *Dearest Enemy*, and with director John Murray Anderson taking over almost at the last minute, the musical opened on Broadway on September 18, 1925. It managed to fool the experts and run for an entire season.

Dearest Enemy showed the kind of daring and imagination that went into almost everything Rodgers and Hart wrote. Not only was its setting unusual for a musical, there was a genuine attempt to make the songs fit the spirit of the time and the place. It had topical references to the New York of the period in "War Is War" and "Where the Hudson River Flows," and even referred to an earlier era in "Sweet Peter," which was about Peter Stuyvesant. "Here In My Arms," "Bye and Bye," and "Here's a Kiss" were romantic expressions that resisted sounding too modern in either their music or their lyrics. On the other hand, the unreal emotions of operetta were also resisted. *Dearest Enemy* proved beyond a doubt that Rodgers and Hart were as skilled in writing a score for a book musical as they had been in creating the songs for a revue.

Rodgers and Hart's attitude toward the theatre was indicated in their attitude toward *Dearest Enemy*. It would have been safer for them to have followed *The Garrick Gaieties* with another intimate revue. Instead, they deliberately chose a subject that experienced men of the theatre had told them would not succeed. This showed a basic feeling that was to be revealed in all of the major Rodgers and Hart and Rodgers and Hammerstein works: Do something because you like it and believe in it, not because you think it will be a hit.

Just four nights after the New York premiere of *Dearest Enemy*, a musical by Oscar Hammerstein, Otto Harbach, and Jerome Kern had *its* premiere. *Sunny* was its name, and it turned out to be almost as successful as *Rose-Marie* had been. But in spite of Hammerstein's lofty dreams of the future of the American musical stage, there was nothing really noteworthy about the show. It was merely a very elaborate, highly entertaining musical that was cut from the same cloth as so many other Broadway spectacles of the time.

Sunny was something of a sequel to *Sally*, a musical that Florenz Ziegfeld had produced five years before. It had the same composer, the same star (Marilyn Miller), and almost the same silly story. This time, however, it was produced by Charles Dillingham.

Co-librettists Harbach and Hammerstein were faced with the problem of writing a book musical as if they were writing a revue. There were so many featured dancers and comics in the show that they were forced to create a story that would not interfere with the specialties. In fact, after Hammerstein had first read an outline of the plot to Marilyn Miller, she had only one question: "When do I do my tap dance?"

That surely isn't the way musicals are put together today. But in the mid-Twenties, little more was needed than attractive songs, spirited dancing, popular stars, and eye-catching scenery and costumes. And *Sunny* easily filled the bill.

Just three months after the opening of *Sunny*, Oscar Hammerstein and Otto Harbach went back to their more familiar type of serious musical play, a tale of the Russian Revolution called *Song of the Flame*. One of the collaborators, Herbert Stothart, was an old friend, but the other composer, George

Gershwin, was a new partner. Gershwin had won fame through his songs for a series of revues called *George White's Scandals*, and had just recently turned to such modern musical comedies as *Lady, Be Good* and *Tip-Toes* (which had opened two nights before the premiere of *Song of the Flame*).

The result of the unusual collaboration of Hammerstein, Harbach, Stothart, and Gershwin was a rather formless work which was neither good operetta nor good musical comedy. However, it did represent—no matter how crudely—Hammerstein's desire to return to the *Wildflower* and *Rose-Marie* type of musical.

That same season, Rodgers and Hart worked on a senseless musical comedy called *The Girl Friend*, which is best remembered for the lovely song of marital happiness, "The Blue Room." Two months later, there was a second edition of *The Garrick Gaieties*. *Gaieties* No. 2 was almost as popular as *Gaieties* No. 1 had been, even though some of the freshness had worn off. There was also a new song in it that was equally as charming as "Manhattan." This was "Mountain Greenery," which described the pleasures city dwellers enjoy during a few weeks' vacation in the country.

The song is an especially good example of the way the lyrics of Lorenz Hart fitted the music of Richard Rodgers. Hart was very fond of tricky rhymes, and Rodgers like to set them to fresh, melodious, but uncomplicated tunes. Had he tried to compose an equally tricky melody, it would have made the combination of words and music too difficult for a listener to fully appreciate. Thus, a rhyme such as "Beans could get no keener reception in a beanery" is effective because the music fits the words instead of competing with them. Actually, what Hart did was to rhyme one word, "beanery," with one and one-third words, "keener re-." This technique of finding the rhyme within a word rather than at the end was a trademark of Larry Hart, and few writers have ever been able to do it more skillfully.

The bright and bubbly musical world of Rodgers and Hart set them apart from most of the writers of the mid-Twenties. Only George and Ira Gershwin and Vincent Youmans with his many collaborators could approach them. The two became further and further separated from the musical world of Oscar Hammerstein.

As if to atone for *Sunny*, Oscar deliberately chose to write operetta rather than musical comedy. For the next few years he was consistent with his aims of bridging the gap between musical comedy and opera. However, the works he turned out were frequently too old-fashioned to be accepted as good examples of either. And for his collaborators, he went to the men who were more comfortable writing in the European tradition than in adjusting themselves to an American musical point of view.

The Wild Rose, with music by Rudolf Friml, came along in October, 1926. *The Desert Song*, with music by Sigmund Romberg, arrived a month later. Both of these works depicted a never-never land of romance that was a little too unreal even for the Twenties. But *The Desert Song*, in spite of its childish plot, did have such an exotic setting that it soon attracted a large audience. It became one of the most successful works of the decade, and is still one of the most frequently revived musicals throughout the country.

Of no little help to *The Desert Song* is its truly beautiful score. The series of soaring melodies never fails to find responsive audiences. They manage to capture the romance and glamour of the Middle East, which is apparently enough to make people accept the many unbelievable things in the story.

The Desert Song taught Oscar Hammerstein an important

lesson. Although he was very careful in what he wrote for the major arias and duets, he felt that it really wasn't necessary to be concerned with the words to the choral numbers, especially those at the beginning of the show. Latecomers would be taking their seats at that time, and who could possibly make out what a group of thirty men were singing about? And who could possibly care? When *The Desert Song* opened in London, however, Hammerstein received a shock. Every clipped word that the expertly drilled men of the chorus were singing could easily be heard and understood. And what they were singing were such amateurish lines as these:

> As we are drinking,
> Merrily drinking,
> Who would be thinking
> Who we are!

Upon hearing the lines, Hammerstein sneaked out of the theatre in embarrassment. From then on, he made certain that no line in a song received anything but his best effort. Years later, he was reminded of this incident when he saw a newspaper photograph of the Statue of Liberty taken from a helicopter. It showed the back of the goddess' head, where the sculpturing was as perfectly done as on any other part of the statue. What a great artist the sculptor Bartholdi was, Hammerstein felt. He never could have dreamed that a photograph could be taken of that part of the statue. Yet because he was such a perfectionist, Bartholdi was unable to do anything sloppy.

If 1926 through 1927 was a period in which Oscar Hammerstein was settling into a creative mold, it was also a period in which Richard Rodgers was striving to express himself through a wide variety of musicals.

During the summer of 1926, Rodgers and Hart took a vacation in Europe. They were also able to combine their travels with an assignment to write a score for an English musical called *Lido Lady*. It had a featherweight story about an English tennis champion (known as the "Lido Lady") whose father is determined that she marry only a man as good at sports as she is. Rodgers and Hart wrote over fifteen new songs for the show. However, the hit number turned out to be "Here In My Arms," which they had borrowed from *Dearest Enemy*.

Back in New York, the team promptly set to work writing the scores for two new musicals that were to open within one day of each other. The first was called *Peggy-Ann*, for which they were joined by their most frequent collaborator, Herbert Fields. The other was *Betsy*, which was produced by Florenz Ziegfeld.

Peggy-Ann was a most unusual musical comedy, a fantasy in which almost all of the action took place in a dream. As if that were not daring enough, it had no opening chorus. Nor was there any singing for the first fifteen minutes. When the chorus girls did come in, they were used as part of the plot rather than as mere ornaments. At the end of the show, after Peggy-Ann finally awakened from her three-hour dream, the scene was played in semidarkness.

These unusual touches were not put in merely to shock audiences. They were all part of the original idea of the play, which was a sort of *Alice In Wonderland* for grownups. Many different things were satirized in *Peggy-Ann*, including musical comedy itself, and the songs were used intelligently to make their own satiric points.

Betsy opened the night after *Peggy-Ann*. Its book was weak, and the songs were not among Rodgers and Hart's best. In fact the song hit was "Blue Skies," which had been written by Irving Berlin.

Rodgers and Hart had returned from their trip to England

even before rehearsals had started for *Lido Lady*. Therefore, curious to see what the show looked like, they sailed again for England in January, 1927. While in London, they agreed to do the score for a new revue to be produced by Charles B. Cochran, the most famous producer of musicals in England. Their show, *One Dam Thing After Another*, opened in London about a month and a half after the English premiere of *The Desert Song*.

Richard Rodgers has never depended upon inspiration for any of his melodies. He has always had to go to work to try to find the right combination of notes for a song that will fit a particular situation. Once, however, he did get an idea for a song from something that actually happened to him. Shortly before *One Dam Thing After Another* opened, Rodgers and Hart were visiting Paris. One day they were in a taxicab with two girls when the cab almost collided with another car. All were somewhat shaken by the experience, and one of the girls gasped, "Oh, my heart stood still!" Hart, who was always on the lookout for an idea for a lyric, quickly forgot what had happened, and remarked, "Say, that's a very good song title." Rodgers made a mental note of it, and when the team returned to London, wrote the melody for the song. Hart knew nothing at all about it until Rodgers showed him the music and said, "Here's the tune for that title of yours." "What title?" asked his partner, who had forgotten the incident. "My Heart Stood Still," Rodgers told him. Hart liked his own title and his partner's music, and promptly went to work to complete the rest of the lyric.

Hart's lyric for "My Heart Stood Still" is especially noteworthy because it combines simplicity with eloquence. Almost as if to prove that he did not always need intricate rhymes, Hart wrote the refrain, or main part of the song, almost entirely with words of only one syllable. The only two-syllable words in it are "single," "spoken," "unfelt," "never," "until," and "moment."

"My Heart Stood Still" became so popular in London that Rodgers and Hart bought it back from Cochran to use again. They didn't have long to wait. In the fall of 1927, it became a hit all over again, but this time in the Broadway show, *A Connecticut Yankee*.

A Connecticut Yankee followed *Peggy-Ann* into the Vanderbilt Theatre, and had an even longer run. Like *Peggy-Ann*, it was a dream fantasy. However, it was based on a completely different idea, Mark Twain's *A Connecticut Yankee At King Arthur's Court*. Ever since they had seen the silent movie version of the book, Rodgers, Hart and Fields had wanted to make a musical out of it. That was in 1921, but they were unable to interest a producer. By 1927, however, after their string of successes, they were able to get Lew Fields and Lyle D. Andrews, the producers of *Peggy-Ann*, to sponsor it.

The mixture of medieval expressions and modern slang gave Rodgers and Hart opportunities to create many clever songs. None, however, proved as durable as "My Heart Stood Still."

A Connecticut Yankee was the first Rodgers and Hart musical to run over 400 performances. It was unquestionably their most successful effort presented during the Twenties.

About this time, Hammerstein was kept equally as busy as Rodgers. After launching *The Desert Song* in London, he returned to New York for two productions in rapid succession. *Golden Dawn*, which opened the same month as *A Connecticut Yankee*, was another unreal operetta. Its main character was a female Tarzan living in Nairobi, Africa. Again Otto Harbach was co-librettist and co-lyricist, and again Herbert Stothart was co-composer. The other composer, however, was new: Emmerich Kalman, who wrote most of the score in his native Vienna.

Although *Golden Dawn* was only a moderate success, it was another attempt in the worthy cause of song and story integration. As in *Rose-Marie*, there was a program note:

> The musical numbers are an integral part of the story as it evolves; and therefore are not listed separately.

Hammerstein's second musical of 1927 opened about a month after *Golden Dawn*. He first knew about it when Jerome Kern called him up one day, and in an excited voice asked, "How would you like to do a show for Ziegfeld? It's got a million-dollar title. It's called *Show Boat*."

CHAPTER 4

Show Boat

O<small>SCAR</small> <small>HAMMERSTEIN'S</small> <small>WORTHY</small> <small>HOPES</small> for the musical theatre were not being realized either by himself or by others. By the fall of 1927, he seemed to be unable to break away from the heavy operetta-type musicals. Then he received the call from Jerome Kern that was to change not only his own future but the future of the American musical theatre.

Kern, of course, was the first major composer to break away from the European operetta past. But throughout the Twenties he had still been unable to follow up his pioneering work with anything more meaningful. And Hammerstein, who had broken away from the silly musical comedy farces, now found himself involved in the kind of musical that had driven Kern to create the daring Princess Theatre musicals.

Both men had discussed this problem many times since their collaboration on *Sunny*. Surely, they maintained, there must be a form of musical theatre that could tell an adult story without relying on the formulas of the past. If possible, they would want to use a story with an American locale. But no matter what the tale would be, it must be strong enough to be worthy of a treatment that would use music as a necessary tool in the telling of the story. Kern and Hammerstein agreed to collaborate on such a property if either one ever found it.

One night Jerome Kern picked up a copy of Edna Ferber's novel, *Show Boat.* Even before he had finished it, he became convinced that here was the perfect story for the musical he wanted to write with Hammerstein. The plot made sense. The locales were colorful. The characters were believable. And it had a great title. Losing no time, Kern bought the stage rights from Edna Ferber, got Hammerstein to agree to collaborate on it, and then talked Florenz Ziegfeld into producing it.

Many people of the theatre thought that Kern and Hammerstein must be crazy to undertake a musical version of *Show Boat.* The plot broke too many rules of what to do and what not to do in writing a successful musical. For one thing, there was the situation of the two unhappy marriages, one of them between a white man and a mulatto woman. For another, the story touched upon the sad lot of Southern Negroes. How could Kern and Hammerstein expect audiences to accept such things in a light musical entertainment? These were real situations existing in the United States. There was no special appeal of a faraway locale to give them romantic quality. It was even more surprising that such a smart showman as Ziegfeld was willing to be its producer.

What audiences saw when *Show Boat* had its world premiere in Washington, D. C., on November 15, 1927, was actually the first modern American musical play. The dramatic conflict was strong enough to be dramatized without music. Yet it was the music of *Show Boat* that enhanced the tale and gave it a deeper meaning. Perhaps more important, audiences accepted it at once. It may have been daring, but even before *Show Boat* dropped anchor at the Ziegfeld Theatre in New

York, there was no question that it would succeed. Ziegfeld had done it again, and Kern and Hammerstein had ushered in a new era in the history of the musical theatre.

As far as Hammerstein was concerned personally, this, at last, was his opportunity to win recognition. It was the thirteenth musical for which he contributed both lyrics and libretto, yet it was the first one since *Always You* that he had written without a collaborator. It proved that he could at last succeed on his own.

In the writing of the songs, Kern and Hammerstein were very careful that each number should have a definite purpose in the story. The lovers, Magnolia and Gaylord, would first find expression in the simple game of pretending, "Make Believe," and later reveal deeper emotions in "Why Do I Love You?" and "You Are Love." The mulatto, Julie (played by Helen Morgan), could pour her heart out in "Can't Help Lovin' Dat Man." The comic character, Ellie, could describe with perfect frankness that "Life Upon the Wicked Stage" is not as glamorous as most girls think.

In some cases it was necessary to use songs that were not specially written for *Show Boat*. For the important New Year's Eve party scene in Chicago, the authors went back to the thirty-five-year-old sentimental ballad "After the Ball" by Charles K. Harris. For a second torch song for Julie, they revived—and revised—"Bill," which Kern and Wodehouse had written for *Oh, Lady! Lady!!* in 1918.

Since they wanted their score to have a unity of style, Kern and Hammerstein used various musical devices to achieve it. Gaylord Ravenal's "Till Good Luck Comes My Way" was a swaggering character song that caught the personality of the riverboat gambler. Yet in one small section, the audience is made to realize that with all his bravado, he has really fallen under the spell of the sweet and simple Magnolia Hawks. This comes when he sings the lines "I let fate decide/ If I walk or ride." These four measures actually repeat four measures that Magnolia had sung as part of their first duet, "Make Believe": "You do not offend/ We only pretend." The writers also used a "Misery Theme" to underline the tragedy of Julie's unhappy life.

Hammerstein, however, was not only concerned with style, he was also concerned with content. For the first time, he had written a libretto and lyrics that would reveal something of the philosophy of Oscar Hammerstein. This was particularly true of the play's handling of the Negro characters. During the Twenties, with rare exceptions, Negroes were treated as comic characters on the musical stage. They were the buffoons, the butts of many tasteless jokes. Hammerstein showed his understanding of their plight right at the beginning of *Show Boat*. When the curtain rises, the Negro dock workers are seen lifting the heavy bales of cotton. Their first song, "Cotton Blossom," is an expression of misery at being forced to do this backbreaking work. Soon, when the town dandies and their ladies come down to the levee, they too sing about the "Cotton Blossom." But while the dock workers continue to sing about the cotton plant, the white townspeople sing the praises of the *Cotton Blossom* showboat.

The one song in *Show Boat* that reveals the most about both Hammerstein's craft and his philosophy is "Ol' Man River." When he and Kern first began to work on *Show Boat*, they found that they would have to write a song that would tie all the sprawling parts of the story together. They found their theme in the Mississippi River, which Edna Ferber had brought into every important turn in the novel. But what kind of river song should it be? Hammerstein thought and thought about this. Finally he decided that instead of giving it to one of the major characters, he would give the song to one of the Negro dock workers.

His song conveys the almost unbearable hopelessness that

the man feels when he compares his life of toil with the easy life of the Mississippi River. The words are simple, even primitive, with very few rhymes. However, the power and nobility of the music and lyric have given it an almost heroic folk quality. At last a Negro on the musical stage was written about with dignity. At last an author's concern for his fellow man could be used logically within the framework of a Broadway musical.

No such towering work as *Show Boat* came from the pens of Rodgers and Hart that season. Yet the Kern and Hammerstein musical did have a great effect on Rodgers. "I think it was the deep impression this piece made on me," he has written, "that sent me to Oscar years later with the suggestion that we might find it advisable to work together."

Rodgers and Hart wrote two minor shows after *A Connecticut Yankee. She's My Baby* had little more than Beatrice Lillie to recommend it. *Present Arms*, three months later, dealt with Marines at Pearl Harbor. Both were formula musicals, occasionally enlivened by the songs.

The fall of 1928 was an especially busy season for Hammerstein. However, he was unable to follow *Show Boat* with anything approaching it in quality. In September, he wrote the book of *Good Boy* with Otto Harbach and Henry Myers. The success of the musical was due more to its use of treadmills for moving the actors from scene to scene than to its story or songs. Later in the same month, Hammerstein was represented by *The New Moon*, for which he was co-librettist and solo lyricist.

The New Moon had much in common with *The Desert Song.* Both musicals were produced by Laurence Schwab and Frank Mandel. Both had music by Sigmund Romberg. Both starred Robert Halliday in the leading roles. Both were vaguely based on historical incidents. And both turned out to be highly successful examples of old-fashioned operetta.

Before it became a success, however, *The New Moon* had to undergo many long months of writing and rewriting. It first opened in Philadelphia in December, 1927, at about the same time as the New York opening of *Show Boat*. After two weeks, it was closed for revisions. In the theatre, this is usually a polite way to say that a show has closed for good. But in the case of *The New Moon*, it was really true. Seven and a half months later, an almost entirely new *New Moon* opened in Cleveland. It then proceeded to New York where its official premiere took place on September 19, 1928. It caught on quickly and had a profitable run of 509 performances.

The score was probably the best one written by Sigmund Romberg and Oscar Hammerstein. Four of its romantic pieces —"Lover, Come Back to Me," "Softly, As In a Morning Sunrise," "Wanting You," and "One Kiss"—are among the most popular love songs ever created for the musical stage. One long-forgotten song, "Love Is Quite a Simple Thing," was always a favorite of Oscar's. In it, he treated the subject of love in a light and offhand manner. Since birds and fish seem to experience love, he argued, it really "ain't no miracle" when a boy and a girl fall in love.

Six days after *The New Moon* opened in New York, Rodgers and Hart's *Chee-Chee* had its New York premiere. The show was a failure, but it is worth noting because it was another serious attempt to make the songs of a musical fit logically into its plot. Like Kern and Hammerstein, Rodgers and Hart had been striving to write a well-integrated musical for a number of years. It was unfortunate that they tried to work out this idea on such an unappealing play as *Chee-Chee*.

What Hart wanted to do in *Chee-Chee*, as he put it, was to "write a new form of musical show which will not be a musical comedy and will not be an operetta." He and Rodgers wanted the songs to be a definite part of the progress of the story, "not extraneous interludes without rhyme or reason." This, of course, was very similar to Hammerstein's long-held view. The program of *Chee-Chee* even carried an explanatory note similar to the ones Hammerstein had written for the programs of *Rose-Marie* and *Golden Dawn*: "The musical numbers, some of them very short, are so interwoven with the story that it would be confusing for the audience to peruse a complete list." It then listed only six songs as being "among the principal musical numbers."

Thus, though the theatre of Richard Rodgers at the time was quite different from the theatre of Oscar Hammerstein, they were both trying to reach the same goals. Except for *Show Boat*, neither writer met with much success in creating this new form of musical theatre. But the important thing is that each man, on his own, was striving to achieve something meaningful and original on the musical stage.

Rainbow, Oscar Hammerstein's next musical, was part of this new movement. Though opening in New York after *The New Moon*, it was clearly intended to follow in the same musical path as *Show Boat*.

True, it was plagued by bad luck almost from the start. However, there were so many good things in *Rainbow* that it is unfortunate it lasted only one month. Like *Show Boat*, it had a realistic, colorful story and an outstanding musical score. But unlike *Show Boat*, this saga of the California Gold Rush of 1849, which Hammerstein wrote with Laurence Stallings, was not put together with the skill that such a production requires. During the tryout tour an argument between producer Philip Goodman and composer Vincent Youmans resulted in the composer taking out all the love songs. What were left were marching songs, comic songs, and torch songs. On opening night, the sets wouldn't operate properly, and a donkey misbehaved on stage. The end of the first act didn't come until about ten minutes to eleven. All these things helped ruin the chances of a frequently bold and original show, with bright dialogue and a score that conveyed the proper spirit of the lusty tale.

The failure of *Rainbow* did not alter Hammerstein's outlook on the musical stage. The failure of *Chee-Chee*, however, seems to have made Rodgers and Hart a bit more cautious. Early in 1929, they wrote the music and lyrics of a conventional musical comedy called *Spring Is Here*. For a plot it had one of the favorite subjects of the musicals of the Twenties: love among the idle rich on Long Island. But the score, including such songs as "With a Song In My Heart" and "Why Can't I?," gave luster to the well-worn situations.

On May 14, 1929, after divorcing his first wife, Oscar Hammerstein married Dorothy Blanchard. The second Mrs. Hammerstein was born in Australia, and had appeared on the New York stage in *André Charlot's Revue of 1925*. After giving up the theatre, she had become an interior decorator.

Almost as soon as his wedding trip was over, Hammerstein plunged into the writing of a new musical. Ever since Helen Morgan had scored a success as Julie in *Show Boat*, Kern and Hammerstein had wanted to write a show just for her. Instead of an adaptation this time, they wrote an original story called *Sweet Adeline*. It opened on Broadway in September, 1929. The tale of the rise of a beer garden singer to a musical comedy star at the turn of the century may not have been very strong, but it allowed the writers to create songs of great atmosphere and period charm. The best-remembered ones, "Don't Ever Leave Me" and "Why Was I Born?," had the proper misty-eyed flavor, but all of the musical numbers were exactly right for the locale and the plot.

The Wall Street crash of 1929 occurred a little more than

a month after the opening of *Sweet Adeline*. The Depression that followed greatly affected the lives of everyone throughout the world. It was also responsible for changes in the theatre, including the musical theatre. *Sweet Adeline* provided a relief from the day's worries, and it lasted until the middle of March.

Rodgers and Hart's next musical, *Heads Up!*, unfortunately had to open in New York just thirteen days after the stock market crash. Yet in spite of the panic that gripped the country at the time, it too ran until the middle of March. Like *Spring Is Here*, it had a conventional plot. The main difference between the two shows was that the idle rich were put on a yacht off New London, Connecticut, rather than on an estate on Long Island. The show concerned itself with the problem of rum-running which, because of Prohibition, was still a topical subject at the time.

Simple Simon, Rodgers and Hart's first musical of the Thirties, was a childish fantasy tailor-made for Ed Wynn. Two incidents connected with the show are good examples of how unpredictable the theatre can be. While *Simple Simon* was giving tryout performances prior to opening in New York, Ruth Etting, the torch singer, was enjoying a personal success on Broadway in the *9:15 Revue*. In spite of her acclaimed performance, however, the show lasted only a week. Once it closed, producer Florenz Ziegfeld hired Miss Etting to replace another actress in *Simple Simon*. Then, with the Broadway opening only one night away, Ziegfeld made Rodgers and Hart write a new song for her. The partners worked all night and came up with the bitter tale of the dance hall hostess, "Ten Cents a Dance." Ruth Etting sang the song opening night without a rehearsal. After she finished, she had scored her second great hit in a row—and it all happened within one month.

The second incident concerned the song "Dancing On the

Ceiling," which Rodgers and Hart had written for *Simple Simon*. Everyone connected with the musical loved that song except producer Florenz Ziegfeld. All of Rodgers and Hart's pleading was to no avail. Ziegfeld didn't like the song, and it couldn't stay in the show. But the writers were so convinced of the merits of "Dancing On the Ceiling" that they put it into the very next musical they wrote. This was a London show called *Ever Green*. Producer Charles Cochran loved the song, and the way Jessie Matthews sang it and danced to it helped make it the hit of the show.

Shortly after *Simple Simon* opened, Richard Rodgers married Dorothy Feiner.

The Feiner family and the Rodgers family had known each other for many years. In fact, Dr. William Rodgers was the Feiners' doctor. Young Dick had first met his future bride when he was seven. He was visiting Dorothy's older brother, Ben, who was then five, and Dorothy was only two months old at the time. In September, 1926, Rodgers met her again. She was on board the ship taking Rodgers and Hart back to New York after they had finished their work for *Lido Lady*. The young couple saw each other as often as her schooling and his work would allow. They were married on March 5, 1930, and spent their wedding trip in Europe.

Rodgers still managed to combine business with pleasure. He and Hart had already agreed to write the score for *Ever Green*, and the newlyweds rented an apartment in London. After getting settled, they invited Larry Hart to stay with them. As soon as the score was finished, the trio sailed for the United States. Something new and challenging had turned up. Hollywood wanted Rodgers and Hart.

CHAPTER 5

To Hollywood and Back

ON THE NIGHT OF October 6, 1927, a revolution took place in New York. It was only the premiere of a new motion picture, but for the first time a sign hung from a theatre marquee that could proclaim: SEE AND HEAR AL JOLSON IN *The Jazz Singer*.

Only a few sequences in *The Jazz Singer* used sound. Yet it was the film that made the biggest impact in the development of the motion picture industry. Before long, movies were being made that were advertised as "All-Talking"—and even "All-Talking, All-Singing, and All-Dancing."

It was only natural that movie executives would want to make musicals, since this was one type of film that had not been suited to the silent screen. And since the studios had no composers and lyricists on hand, they did two things: they filmed already successful Broadway musicals, and they began signing up songwriters to create original musicals especially for the "talkies."

The first Hammerstein musical adapted for the screen was
Rose-Marie, which was released in February, 1928. This was
a silent film featuring Joan Crawford, though a recorded score
was sent out to accompany it. In May the following year, both
The Desert Song and *Show Boat* were released. *The Desert
Song* was a hit, but *Show Boat* ran into special difficulties. Its
producer, Carl Laemmle, had no faith in sound and had actually begun the film as a silent. Midway during the shooting,
however, he added a few talking sequences and tacked on a
"prologue" with performers from the original stage production singing five of the songs. By 1930, however, one movie
musical almost followed another, frequently with greatly altered plots and additional songs by some of the early songwriters to settle in Hollywood. During that year alone, Oscar
Hammerstein's stage musicals had inspired five films: *Song of
the West* (the new title for *Rainbow*); *Song of the Flame;
Golden Dawn; New Moon;* and *Sunny.* Rodgers' shows had
also inspired the same number of films: *The Melody Man;
Spring Is Here* (though there is no record of this movie having played anywhere); *Leathernecking* (the new title for *Present Arms*); and *Heads Up!*

Since motion picture executives were so fond of the original works of Oscar Hammerstein and Richard Rodgers (with
their respective partners), it was only logical that they would
want them—as well as many other successful stage writers—
to create original musicals for the screen. And Hammerstein
was one of the very first to go.

He really had everything to gain and little to lose. In the
depths of the Depression, Warner Brothers offered him and
Sigmund Romberg a most attractive contract. They were to
write four original film musicals in two years for which they
would each be paid $100,000 per film. In addition, the company
gave the composer and lyricist the right to approve the final
casts, scripts, scoring, and even settings. This was surely a

golden opportunity to do something worthwhile in an exciting new medium, and both Romberg and Hammerstein eagerly accepted the offer.

The first product of this collaboration was a film called *Viennese Nights*. It opened in November, 1930, as a reserved-seat attraction at the Warner Theatre in New York City. The producers were so proud of having acquired such distinguished writers that they took the unusual step of having the ads for the film feature photographs of Romberg and Hammerstein rather than the stars. The story, unfortunately, did not really justify this faith. It told an old-fashioned, unbelievable tale of unrequited love, covering three generations of lovers. The movie, however, did have the honor of being the first to present a full symphony orchestra on the screen.

Rodgers, Hart and Fields also went to Hollywood in 1930. Their first original film, *The Hot Heiress*, was far less ambitious than *Viennese Nights*, and it was equally unsuccessful.

The writers were not very happy working on this film. Accustomed to the frantic pace of the Broadway theatre, they felt uncomfortable in the leisurely atmosphere of California. Rodgers and Hart were told that instead of writing for singers, they were to write for the camera. They were advised to take their time, and to enjoy themselves. This was obviously not their kind of theatre.

The experience, however, did serve one good purpose: it provided Rodgers, Hart and Fields with an idea for a Broadway musical comedy. Their show, which opened in February, 1931, was called *America's Sweetheart*. Ann Sothern (then known as Harriette Lake) and Jack Whiting had the leading parts. *America's Sweetheart* made fun of many of the stock characters and situations of film making—the rising star, the fading star, the talkie revolution, the powerful film executives, the fan magazines. Throughout, the score maintained a bright, up-to-the-minute point of view. Even the main romantic duet, "I've Got Five Dollars," took its inspiration from the headlines: it was the Depression that had left the hero and heroine with only five dollars—plus assorted minor possessions—to give to each other as presents.

The great number of movie musicals released in 1930 could have only one result. The public quickly tired of this form of screen entertainment. But Romberg and Hammerstein still had their contract to fulfill. Their second original musical, *Children of Dreams*, was another sentimental romance, though it did have a happy ending. By the time it was released, however, the producer could not even find a first-run movie house to book it. It did even worse business than *Viennese Nights*, and Warner Brothers were glad to pay Romberg and Hammerstein $100,000 each *not* to make the two remaining films in their contract.

About the time that Romberg and Hammerstein returned to New York, Rodgers and Hart again gave in to the financial lure of Hollywood. This was understandable since Rodgers was now a father, and was well aware of his family responsibilities. The theatre was his first love, of course, and he hoped to return to it. But the Depression had made it even more undependable than usual. Rodgers and Hart had written nineteen shows together, but not all of them had turned out to be box-office successes. Despite Rodgers' experience with *The Hot Heiress*, Hollywood was still a challenge, and, what was even more important, one that the composer could meet with a feeling of financial security.

During their early years in Hollywood, Rodgers and Hart worked on films that attempted to break away from the conventions of most movie musicals. This was achieved through a closer integration of music, action, and dialogue. In their film *Love Me Tonight*, the passage of time and locale was bridged by various people singing one song, "Isn't It Romantic?" with specially written lyrics to make it appropriate to the story. In *The Phantom President*, which starred George M. Cohan, they had occasional bits of dialogue spoken in rhyme. This technique, called "rhythmic dialogue," was used to an even greater degree in *Hallelujah, I'm a Bum!*, starring Al Jolson.

Hallelujah, I'm a Bum! had entire sequences spoken in rhyming couplets so that it was completely logical whenever one of the characters burst into an actual song. Just as Rodgers and Hart had worked toward a closer blending of song and story on the stage, so their first motion picture scores were concerned with telling a story through music and lyrics. It was a fresh, original touch that has become more appreciated in later years than it was at the time the films were made. This was mainly due to something no one could overlook: only one of the films, *Love Me Tonight*, did well at the box office, and that may well have been because of the popularity of its star, Maurice Chevalier.

Hammerstein's first shows on his return to New York were not marked by success either. *Free for All*, on which he collaborated with composer Richard A. Whiting for the first and only time, was a satire about college students who set up a Socialist community. It was a momentary change from Hammerstein's almost unbroken chain of operettas, and it startled many by not having the customary chorus line.

Free for All was quickly followed by *East Wind*. Oscar Hammerstein was now in more familiar operetta surroundings. The musical reunited him with Sigmund Romberg to create a tale of romance and adventure in such colorful locales as Marseilles and Indochina. Nevertheless, the situations and characters were so dated that the show didn't even last a month.

Counting his two films, Hammerstein now had four failures in a row. The area in which he felt most comfortable—operetta—was almost a thing of the past. The new style political satires of the Depression years were foreign to Hammerstein's nature. He had to strike out on a new path. And, as before, he struck out on this path with Jerome Kern.

Although Jerome Kern had pioneered the modern musical comedy, he too was unable to adapt himself to writing satirical musicals in the style of the Gershwin brothers' *Of Thee I Sing* or Irving Berlin's *Face the Music*. In 1931, he had turned his back on the modern trend to write the score for *The Cat and the Fiddle* with Otto Harbach. The story was set in Europe, but it was not concerned with international politics or anything timely. It was merely a simple backstage story that used music as a very important part of the plot. Atmosphere, story and characters were all enhanced not only by song but by the steady flow of background music.

This was the kind of musical that Kern and Hammerstein planned to write together. Although it did not imitate the Kern-Harbach musical, in many ways the Kern-Hammerstein musical, *Music In the Air*, was quite similar to *The Cat and the Fiddle*. It was also set in modern Europe (Bavaria instead of Brussels). It also had a backstage story. It also avoided political overtones. And the music was also a necessary part of the plot. Like *The Cat and the Fiddle*, it made no attempt at being up-to-date yet *Music In the Air* turned out to be both timely and timeless.

Oscar Hammerstein was always very fond of *Music In the Air*. It is not hard to see why. In its sentimental story full of the joys of country living, it revealed an attitude that was a very real part of the author's outlook. Hammerstein always believed in the goodness of simple life. His love of nature, first apparent during his summers at Weingart's Institute, never left him. And seldom before had he been able to express this love to the extent that he did in *Music In the Air.*

But there was always a practical side to Oscar Hammerstein and this too was shown in *Music In the Air.* Even though the theatre never ceased to cast a magic spell over him, he was too experienced to have any romantic notions about it. It was because of his deep love for the theatre that he resented such clichés as the inexperienced young girl becoming a star overnight, or the theatre always being a gay, glamorous place in which to work. He knew better. He knew that success comes only to those who work hard; that nothing really worth achieving is easy. All this he put into *Music In the Air.* The sweet country maid who trills so prettily does not replace the aging star of a big musical, simply because youth and ambition are no substitution for experience. The girl is made to realize —after a humiliating scene with the musical's director—that the best place for her is the fresh, free air of her mountain village. And, of course, it is there that she does find true happiness.

As in *The Cat and the Fiddle,* the music and lyrics of *Music In the Air* were inseparable from the story. In addition, the play made great strides in using a technique similar to the rhythmic dialogue Rodgers and Hart were then experimenting with in the movies. This helped place the emphasis where it belonged—on the music. And it also helped the songs spring naturally from the dialogue.

The individual songs in *Music In the Air* were almost equal in quality to those that Kern and Hammerstein had written for *Show Boat.* They had simplicity and charm without ever becoming too sentimental. The lyrics combined Hammerstein's love of nature and music. "In Egern By the Tegern See," which was sung by the elderly wife of a theatrical impressario, is a touching picture of the contentment that is found only in the country as two happy people "watch the sunset fade and melt in the gloam." The shy young lovers from the country, Karl and Sieglinde, reveal their feelings for each other by using references to nature in "I've Told Every Little Star." They confess that they have told the stars and the ripples in a brook about their love, but are just too timid to tell it to each other. In the mountaineers' hiking song, "There's a Hill Beyond a Hill," the townspeople sing of the joys of walking along the open road and climbing mountain after mountain. Again, in the beautiful "And Love Was Born," we are told that the birth of love took place when "a warm spring night was stirred by a breeze" and "a moon in flight was caught in the trees."

The influence of music is brought out in the aria "The Song Is You," in which a worldly Munich playwright proclaims "I hear music when I look at you" as he serenades the star of his show. And Karl and Sieglinde, after their adventures in Munich are over, sing that life is a song now that they will never be parted again ("We Belong Together").

The success of *Music In the Air* led to an English production of the musical just six months after the New York opening. After the London premiere, Hammerstein remained in that city to adapt a German operetta, *Ball at the Savoy*, which had music by Paul Abraham. This was one of the most lavish productions ever seen at the famous old Theatre Royal in Drury Lane. But the musty story, which slightly resembled Johann Strauss' *Die Fledermaus*, was too difficult a hurdle. The show lasted only four months.

Hammerstein loved working in London. He stayed on to write *Three Sisters*, an original musical, with Jerome Kern, which was also presented at the Drury Lane. Though the show's book was rather awkward, it did have some lovely songs. Two of them, "I Won't Dance" and "Lonely Feet," were later used in American movies. But *Three Sisters* ran for only two months.

With two failures in a row in London, Hammerstein had

little choice but to journey to Hollywood once more. His assignment: the lyrics for *The Night Is Young*, another sentimental movie operetta about Old Vienna.

Hammerstein and composer Sigmund Romberg wrote seven songs for the film, including the waltz "When I Grow Too Old to Dream." With its appealing melody and touching words, the song has become one of Romberg's and Hammerstein's most enduring works. However, the lyricist was never entirely pleased with his own efforts. To match the simple form of the music, Hammerstein had to create only eight lines for the refrain, or main part of the song. It took him three weeks to write these few words. The music suggested the first line, which also served as the title. Though he liked the phrase "When I grow too old to dream" when he had first written it, Hammerstein wasn't sure that it made sense. How could a person ever get too old to dream? But the more he tried other lines, the more he kept coming back to that original idea. Then he realized what he was trying to say. The "dream" of the title did not refer to actual dreaming, or reminiscing about the past. What Hammerstein was saying was that when a person can no longer have any hope of loving someone, he will still have the memory of a love that has passed. In spite of the lyricist's concern, however, his meaning has been apparently understood well enough to make the song the standard that it is.

The years 1934 and 1935 were as low for Rodgers as they were for Hammerstein. Of the assorted movies that Rodgers and Hart worked on since *Hallelujah, I'm a Bum!*, none had anything of the originality of their earliest efforts. Life in Hollywood had slowed them down. It had sapped them of their energy to create meaningful works. Their songs of the period were just as attractive as any they had written, but there was little that was inspiring in their film assignments. Both men were becoming more and more unhappy with their unproductive way of life. Possibly they might have remained in Hollywood for a few more years, but one thing made them open their eyes. Glancing through a newspaper one day, Rodgers was attracted to a brief item in a column written by O. O. McIntyre. It was a simple question: "Whatever became of Rodgers and Hart?"

That did it. Just as soon as their contract expired, Rodgers and Hart took the next train heading East.

The New York they returned to early in 1934 only confirmed McIntyre's question. Producers *had* forgotten Rodgers and Hart. Since their last Broadway show, *America's Sweetheart*, had closed in June, 1931, the team had been unrepresented in the musical theatre. Now, almost three years later, they found there was no one to listen to their songs or their ideas. Broadway producers had become far more cautious—remember this was during the Depression—and they had no time for new ideas. Particularly new ideas by a couple of has-beens.

Rodgers and Hart had to wait more than a year and a half before they were given the chance to write a score. Billy Rose, a producer and occasional lyric writer himself, had known and admired Rodgers and Hart for a long time. In 1926, he had hired them to supply the score for a revue at his short-lived night club, the Fifth Avenue Club. Nothing had happened to make him lose faith in their talents, and he was very anxious to have them write the songs for a gigantic new musical he was producing. It was called *Jumbo*.

The show, part musical comedy, part circus, was to be presented at the Hippodrome Theatre, which had long been the showplace for stage spectaculars. Charles MacArthur and Ben Hecht were signed to write the story, John Murray Anderson was to stage the production, and George Abbott would direct the book.

Since this was still a musical production and not merely an imitation circus, every one of the acts had to be carefully trained. And this training took time and money. *Jumbo* was forced to postpone its opening five times. Finally, its gala premiere took place on November 16, 1935. What audiences were treated to was an entirely altered theatre that was rebuilt to look like a real circus tent. There were clowns, jugglers, freaks, Jimmy Durante, and Paul Whiteman on a white horse. Some fifty trained aerialists performed high above the spectators, and there was a menagerie which contained about as many animals.

Jumbo was worth waiting for. And so were the songs by Rodgers and Hart. The warm melodies and the bright lyrics again made people marvel at how perfectly they were suited to each other. In fact, something new had been added. While Hart had always been a master of the clever rhyme, he now showed an even deeper emotion in his lyrics. The touching simplicity of "Little Girl Blue" is a rare example of a popular song catching just the right mood of a lonely, rejected girl sitting in the rain. In "My Romance," Hart approached the eternal subject of love by detailing all the expected romantic accompaniments—such as moon in the sky or a blue lagoon standing by—that are really unnecessary when two people are really in love. Here the lilting melody conveys perfectly the bright-eyed, unsentimental attitude of the lyric, building up to the emotion of the line: "Wide awake I can see my most fantastic dreams come true."

Though *Jumbo* was not a financial success, it did serve well enough to put Rodgers and Hart back on top. Suddenly, it was as if they had never been away. Again Rodgers, now thirty-three, and Hart, now forty, were the most sought-after songwriters in the musical theatre. From then on, their career was an almost unbroken parade of one hit after another.

The good fortune that Richard Rodgers was enjoying during the latter half of the 1930s was nowhere to be found in the vicinity of Oscar Hammerstein. Once Rodgers had returned to New York, he had been able to rid himself of the necessity of writing for the movies. Hammerstein found himself in no such happy situation. Throughout the remainder of the decade, he was continually crisscrossing the continent, hopping from stage assignment to movie assignment and back again.

Just three weeks after the opening of *Jumbo*, Hammerstein was represented on Broadway by *May Wine*, his first stage musical in three years. For the seventh time in his career, he had Sigmund Romberg as his collaborator. This time, however, Hammerstein was not responsible for the story.

May Wine, though it was in many ways a formula operetta of marital misunderstanding in Old Vienna, did have some interesting innovations in stagecraft. It achieved the atmosphere of an intimate operetta by doing away with the chorus. Its music and lyrics—as in *Music In the Air*—were meant to serve an important part in the story, though with less success. But while its intentions may have been worthy, *May Wine* was hindered by a heavy book and a lack of unified style. In fact, it was the melodious score and the intelligent lyrics that were mostly responsible for the musical's popularity.

Soon after the opening of *May Wine*, Hammerstein was off again to the comfortable, profitable, but far from satisfying grind of movie making.

CHAPTER 6

The Late Thirties

THE PERIOD FROM 1936 to 1940 could well be called the "Golden Age of Rodgers and Hart." It was also the lowest point in the career of Oscar Hammerstein.

From April, 1936, through December, 1940, Rodgers and Hart were responsible for the scores of eight Broadway productions, all of which revealed either new facets of their songwriting art or made daring changes in the structure of the musical theatre. Almost everything that the partners touched was both successful at the box office and outstanding artistically. They set the pace for originality on Broadway. During this same period, Hammerstein wrote only one Broadway musical, and that was a failure. For the rest of the time, he turned out scripts and songs for the movies, collaborated on the score for a summer theatre musical, directed and produced three unsuccessful plays in New York, and did the book and lyrics for a pageant at the New York World's Fair.

The 1930s were years of experimentation on Broadway.

From the Depression to the Second World War, the musical theatre—just as the entire country—was awakening to its responsibilities. In stagecraft and in subject matter, it was continually offering brave new ideas. After their political satires, the Gershwin brothers (with DuBose Heyward) had offered a folk opera, *Porgy and Bess*. Harold Rome's revue, *Pins and Needles*, showed that there could be fun in the labor movement, while Marc Blitzstein's *The Cradle Will Rock* used the entire capitalistic system as its target. E. Y. Harburg and Harold Arlen could even spoof international diplomacy in *Hooray for What!* In both *Johnny Johnson* and *Knickerbocker Holiday*, Kurt Weill and his collaborators on each, Paul Green and Maxwell Anderson, tried to say something important about the evils of war and of dictatorship. Of course, the majority of musicals during the Thirties were still concerned with light themes, but even they revealed some of the stirrings then going on in the commercial musical theatre.

Rodgers and Hart were stimulated by what was taking place all around them. But they were leaders, not followers. They didn't even copy themselves. If a show was a success, that was all the more reason for trying something different the next time. Every project was not only a new challenge but a different challenge. And the successes that Rodgers and Hart achieved justified their long-standing belief: the only formula to follow is not to have a formula.

Right after *Jumbo*, Rodgers and Hart created one of the most original musicals of the Thirties, *On Your Toes*. For the show, they dreamed up the story together and even decided to become their own librettists. This, they felt, would give their production a greater unity. However, because of their lack of experience, they soon turned to George Abbott to work with them on the story.

Since *On Your Toes* was all about a former vaudeville hoofer who becomes involved with a ballet company, it gave the writers a wonderful chance to try something new in the musical theatre. They would use ballet sequences as part of the actual story. For their dance director they chose George Balanchine, one of the outstanding ballet choreographers in the world, who had never worked on a musical comedy before. After Balanchine was signed, Rodgers was a bit unsure of how they were to coordinate their work. He asked the Russian-born director, "Do you do the step first, and then I fit the music to it?" "You write," Balanchine commanded. "I make."

One of the most dramatic things that Rodgers wrote and Balanchine made was the ballet "Slaughter On Tenth Avenue." What was even more important, it provided the climax to the actual story. Because another dancer is unable to appear in the ballet, the hoofer (played by Ray Bolger) is forced to substitute. Unknown to him, gangsters are planning to shoot the other dancer because of gambling debts, and the murder is to take place during the dance. Thus, when the hoofer becomes aware of the gangsters sitting in a theatre box, he keeps on dancing to avoid being a target. Luckily, the police arrive just in time to save him.

In this way Rodgers and Balanchine used a complete ballet sequence as something more than a separate episode. Without the dance, there could have been no ending to the play *On Your Toes*. Outstanding though the ballet may have been as an individual dance drama, it took on even greater excitement as a necessary part of the entire story.

Although not all the numbers were as skillfully integrated, the score contained many examples of the way Rodgers and Hart could explore new paths. In "Glad to Be Unhappy," they dealt with the unique situation of a girl taking pleasure in her own misery. In "There's a Small Hotel" (originally written for *Jumbo*), they had their lovers describe their ideal place as a simple country inn, rather than the usual Shangri-la or castle in Spain. And in "It's Gotta Be Love," they compared falling in love to such unromantic ailments as bronchitis, neuritis, and the aftereffects of eating pickles and pie à la mode. In every case the wit of the lyrics was matched by the buoyancy and freshness of the music.

The same month that *On Your Toes* opened, Universal Pictures released its second film version of *Show Boat*. It was a notable production chiefly because Oscar Hammerstein was finally called upon to make his own adaptation of one of his stage works. Also helping to preserve the flavor of the original production were such stage veterans as Irene Dunne (she had been the understudy to the first Magnolia in 1927), Helen Morgan, Paul Robeson, and Charles Winninger.

Because of the success of the film, Hammerstein and Kern convinced the powers at Paramount Pictures that they should be given the opportunity of creating an original film musical. This became *High, Wide and Handsome*. The movie told about the discovery of oil in Pennsylvania just before the Civil War, and the score perfectly suited the atmosphere and the story. Irene Dunne again played a Kern and Hammerstein heroine.

The movie's theme, "The Folks Who Live On the Hill," beautifully summarized the attitude of Hammerstein's two leading characters. Though the hero and heroine have become rich because of discovering the oil on their property, they do not find happiness merely in having money. All they really want out of life is to be able to build their own home and be known as "the folks who live on the hill." The warm contentment here—similar to that of "In Egern on the Tegern See"—is found by two people in love being close to each other surrounded by the beauties of nature.

In spite of many admirable things in it, *High, Wide and*

Handsome struck many as being too much of a horse opera with music, and did poorly at the box office.

Rodgers and Hart's *On Your Toes* had been a great box-office hit. Because of this, its producer, Dwight Deere Wiman, signed the partners to write *Babes In Arms* for him the following spring, and he again had Balanchine create the dances. This time, confident of their own ability to write a story without any assistance, they took sole responsibility for the plot.

The story had a serviceable enough idea. Its tale of youngsters putting on their own musical show gave the authors plenty of opportunity to integrate songs into both the story and the story within the story. The special charm of *Babes In Arms* was that it seemed to have actually been put together by the same kind of stagestruck kids who had created *The Garrick Gaieties.*

Rodgers and Hart's aim was to make every number part of the plot. But this did not stop *Babes In Arms* from having more long-lasting hit songs than any of the team's other musicals. Almost every number produced something original in words and in music. "My Funny Valentine," a love song to a less-than-perfect physical specimen, used the sincerity of the melody to bring out the true feelings of the rather uncomplimentary lyric. The song was originally sung by Mitzi Green to Ray Heatherton, who played the role of a young man whose name really was Valentine. Another interesting contrast in words and music was found in "I Wish I Were In Love Again." Here the exciting music helped put across the notion that being in love was really worthwhile, despite all the fighting that goes with it.

"Where Or When" was certainly among the most original songs ever written. It explored the strange feeling that people sometimes get that they are reliving experiences that they had before—even though they are having these experiences for the very first time. Rodgers matched Hart's remarkable lyric with an equally remarkable melody that had the proper feeling of delicacy and fantasy. The robust number "The Lady Is a Tramp" proclaimed the strong beliefs of the unconventional female who dared to be different. Yet in spite of the girl's declaration that Hobohemia is the place for her, the point of the song is that the young lady really leads a very normal life. She merely refuses to do the unkind and unthoughtful things that all of her friends are doing. "Johnny One Note," another inspired creation, related the saga of a vocal freak whose one note was so piercing that it could silence animals, thunderclaps, traffic, Niagara Falls, and every kind of whistle.

During the Thirties, many writers for the musical stage favored political subjects. Among the most memorable of these shows were *Strike Up the Band, Of Thee I Sing, Let 'Em Eat Cake, Face the Music,* and *As Thousands Cheer.* In 1937, George S. Kaufman, who had co-authored the first three, and Moss Hart, who had written the last two, joined for a new political satire, *I'd Rather Be Right.* This promised to be the most daring idea of all: a lampoon of President Franklin D. Roosevelt, with the actors playing the parts of living people.

Rodgers and Hart were intrigued by the boldness of the idea. The main problem was in casting. Who could play Roosevelt? All four writers were agreed that the only actor for the part was George M. Cohan. But Cohan, who was then almost sixty, was in semiretirement. Although he had won fame in the early years of the century as the theatre's outstanding song-and-dance man, he had not appeared in a Broadway musical in almost ten years. Furthermore, he had serious doubts that he could play the part. Cohan did yield eventually, and he gave an outstanding performance. Nevertheless, he was extremely unhappy during all the months that he appeared in *I'd Rather Be Right,* chiefly because it was the first musical he had ever appeared in that he had not written himself. Because of this, he took out most of his unhappiness on Rodgers and Hart.

One of Rodgers' blackest days in the theatre occurred when he arranged to play the score for Cohan. Rodgers' friend Jules Glaenzer had an apartment with two pianos, and he gladly gave his permission to use his home for the audition. With the producer, Sam Harris, and Kaufman and Hart also there, Rodgers and his rehearsal pianist, Margot Hopkins, played the score. Larry Hart helped out with the singing. All the while, Cohan sat completely motionless in a chair between the two pianos. He didn't budge or say a word. Then, after Rodgers had finished, Cohan slowly rose, patted the composer on the shoulder and said, "Don't take any wooden nickels." Then he walked out of the house without saying another word.

This set the tone of the relationship between George M. Cohan and Rodgers and Hart. In Boston during the tryout, the star refused to sing a line about his friend Al Smith because he felt it was uncomplimentary. Hart had to change the line. Cohan never even referred to Rodgers and Hart by name, but always called them "Gilbert and Sullivan." He frequently would say to someone in the company, "Tell Gilbert and Sullivan to go back to their hotel and write me a better song."

Such friction between the star and the composer and lyricist only gave the show more publicity. Even without it, the fact that George M. Cohan was playing Franklin D. Roosevelt was enough to keep the newspaper columns crowded with items for weeks. This helped to give *I'd Rather Be Right* a ticket sale of about $300,000 even before the show opened on Broadway. This was the largest advance sale up to that time, though today it would be considered very little.

I'd Rather Be Right opened in November, 1937, and ran until June of the following year. It then toured for about six months beginning in the fall. The story of the musical used the convenient device of having a young man fall asleep in New York's Central Park and dream that President Roosevelt personally helps him make up his mind about marrying his sweetheart. Many jokes were made at the expense of the New Deal, the W.P.A., the Cabinet, the Supreme Court, and other institutions. Cohan scored a personal success in spite of his attitude toward the play, though the contributions of Rodgers and Hart may have suffered from their relationship with Cohan.

In general, the satirical nature of the show forced Rodgers and Hart to come up with a score that did not display their natural gifts at their best. The songs fitted the situations and had the right point of view, but there were few with enough melodic appeal to stand out. Hart wrote some witty lines for the members of the Cabinet to sing during a meeting, and for a Presidential press conference in which Roosevelt dishes out some scandal "Off The Record." There was only one romantic song, "Have You Met Miss Jones?," but its beautiful melody was not helped by a strangely awkward lyric.

After a brief trip to Hollywood to write songs for the film *Fools for Scandal*, Rodgers and Hart returned to New York to create the book and score for another Broadway triumph, *I Married an Angel*. The story of the show, like the one for *On Your Toes*, had originally been planned for the movies. Since nothing had been done about it, the partners had little difficulty in persuading Dwight Deere Wiman to produce it as his third annual Rodgers and Hart spring musical. As in the first two, *On Your Toes* and *Babes In Arms*, the choreography was staged by George Balanchine.

Again Rodgers and Hart dared to be different. Fantasies on the musical stage have always been hard to do successfully. But this one was not only a fantasy, it was also a very sophisticated one. Based on a Hungarian play, it told of a wealthy banker (played by Dennis King) who vows that he will marry only a real angel (Vera Zorina), and the complications that arise when this actually comes true.

Since Zorina was a trained ballet dancer, *I Married an Angel* was able to make further strides in integrating ballet into the story of a musical comedy. The highlights were the elaborate "Honeymoon Ballet" and the burlesque of a typical stage show then featured at the Roxy Theatre and the Radio City Music Hall. There were also episodes in which Rodgers and Hart went back to the technique of rhythmic dialogue, which they had first tried out in the movies. This made it easy for the songs to flow naturally from the spoken dialogue, since the dialogue was often accompanied by a musical background.

One of the most touching pieces in the score of *I Married an Angel* was the self-pitying "Spring Is Here." Again Rodgers and Hart showed their brilliant use of contrast: the beauties of the traditional season for lovers mean little to one who is unloved.

Many people have found clues to Lorenz Hart's personality in such expressions as "Spring Is Here" and "Glad to Be Unhappy." For Hart was a very strange and lonely man. He was self-conscious about his short height and what he felt was his unattractive appearance. Even as a young man he drank heavily. Despite his great talent, he never really enjoyed writing, and as the years went by, it became increasingly hard for him to apply himself to his work. He would disappear for weeks in the middle of writing a new score, only to return as mysteriously as he had left.

The problem of writing with Larry Hart was balanced by the fact that he was a very kind and good person. And he was unquestionably among the top lyric writers in the theatre. His own personal problems were doubtlessly responsible for the growing maturity in his work. Always a skilled rhymer, he became less and less concerned with tricky rhymes for their own sake, and more and more concerned with the meaning of a song. In the simple, direct statement of "Spring Is Here," it could very well have been Larry Hart himself wondering aloud about his loneliness. "No desire, no ambition leads me/ Maybe it's because nobody needs me" were two revealing lines in the song. No matter what Rodgers and others would do to make him feel needed and loved, Hart always felt as if he were an outsider.

In the summer of 1938, Rodgers' future partner, Oscar Hammerstein, was trying out a new musical in the hope of getting back to Broadway. It was called *Gentlemen Unafraid*, but its only professional showing was one week at the St. Louis Municipal Opera. With his old collaborator Otto Harbach as co-lyricist and co-librettist, and with Jerome Kern supplying the music, Hammerstein felt confident that his run of bad luck would now be ended. But the show unfortunately was merely another attempt at the kind of musical better suited to the bygone days of Victor Herbert. *Gentlemen Unafraid* never made it to New York.

Though this was a bitter disappointment to Hammerstein, he was still determined to do something in the legitimate theatre. He did return in the fall of 1938, but none of the three productions he worked on was a success. Nor was he credited with writing any of them.

For Laurence Schwab, who had produced some of his earlier hits, Hammerstein directed a biographical play about Gilbert and Sullivan. It was called *Knights of Song*, and it ran for only 16 performances. One month later, Hammerstein co-produced *Where Do We Go From Here?*, a straight play which lasted just one performance less. What is interesting about this play, though, is that it dealt with the theme of brotherhood, a subject that would become more and more important to Hammerstein in his musicals with Rodgers. Just eleven days after *Where Do We Go From Here?* opened, another Hammerstein production, *Glorious Morning*, was unveiled. This one played only nine performances. Nevertheless, the play revealed something of Hammerstein's broadening interest. It was a retelling of the Joan of Arc legend in modern terms so that it applied to the struggle against dictatorship.

The same week that *Glorious Morning* was eking out its brief run, a first-night audience was attending the premiere of a new Rodgers and Hart musical, *The Boys from Syracuse*.

Rodgers first thought of the idea for *The Boys from Syracuse* when he and his partner were on their way to Atlantic City to work on *I Married an Angel*. Since Shakespeare was the greatest playwright of all times, it seemed strange to him that no one had ever thought of doing a musical version of one of the Bard's comedies. The mere novelty of the idea immediately caught Hart's fancy. *The Comedy of Errors* seemed like a natural to both men because the leading comic roles of the twin Dromios would be so easy to cast. Hart's brother, Teddy Hart, who was a very good comedian, was constantly being mistaken for another comic, Jimmy Savo. Here would be a great opportunity to take advantage of their resemblance, and the men were signed just as soon as *I Married an Angel* had been successfully launched on Broadway.

George Abbott wrote the book of *The Boys from Syracuse*, and managed to remove all of Shakespeare's lines with the exception of "The venom clamours of a jealous woman poisons more deadly than a mad dog's tooth." The reading of this line was followed by Mr. Savo stepping to the footlights and confiding to the audience the identity of the line's author.

Rodgers and Hart's contributions were remarkable for their melodic quality and their wit. Again Hart showed his great ability at dealing with opposites to reveal an emotion. Just as "It's Gotta Be Love" in *On Your Toes* compared love to physical ailments, so "This Can't Be Love" in *The Boys from*

Syracuse now expressed doubt that it really could be true love since the emotion was not accompanied by the customary sighs, sorrows, or sobs. In a line from the song "My heart does not stand still," Hart deliberately denied a symptom that he had once used to describe love in an earlier lyric.

"Falling In Love With Love" had one of Rodgers' most haunting waltz melodies, to which Hart added a lyric of great eloquence. The delicacy of the music was perfect for the Grecian setting of the play, and so were "You Have Cast Your Shadow On the Sea" and "The Shortest Day of the Year."

Although there were many attractive things in it, Rodgers and Hart's next musical, *Too Many Girls*, had far fewer surprises than anything else the team had done recently. It was a typical collegiate musical which gained much from George Abbott's swift-paced direction, but showed little interest in an intelligent plot or in well-integrated songs.

Too Many Girls opened in New York in October, 1939. During the following month, Rodgers was represented by his first complete ballet and Hammerstein was represented by his first Broadway musical in four years. The Rodgers assignment, called *Ghost Town*, was commissioned by the Ballet Russe de Monte Carlo, and it was presented for five performances at the Metropolitan Opera House. Not only the form but the subject matter was new to the composer. Creating a score to bring out the flavor of a gold-mining town in the Old West required him to attempt a folk quality in his music. This very same quality, of course, was to turn up three and a half years later in *Oklahoma!*

The name of the Oscar Hammerstein musical presented the same month was *Very Warm For May*. If the choice of subject matter for Rodgers' ballet was somewhat in the Americana vein of such Hammerstein works as *Rainbow* and *High, Wide and Handsome*, so Hammerstein's new work had something of the flavor of Rodgers and Hart's *Babes In Arms*. In it, Hammerstein told of the adventures of a group of young, ambitious actors who toil at a very progressive summer barn theatre. Its aim was satirical and its target was the kind of experimental theatre that is more arty than art. Unfortunately, Hammerstein was unable to create a logical plot that expressed his feelings in an entertaining manner.

Very Warm For May not only brought Oscar Hammerstein back to Broadway, it also brought back Jerome Kern, who had been away for an even longer period of time. Though the combination of Kern and Hammerstein did not result in a successful musical, it did result in an especially lovely score. Kern's music was just as warm, just as overflowing with rich melody as it had ever been. The lyrics, however, were somewhat more sophisticated than Hammerstein's customary work. "That Lucky Fellow" was a love song for a modern suburban couple. "All In Fun" detailed the way a blasé socialite found herself falling in love despite her vow to keep things from getting serious.

The most durable piece in the score was "All the Things You Are," which was sung by a minor member of the cast as part of a show in rehearsal at the barn. The exquisite melody inspired a more personal and poetic lyric from Hammerstein than he wrote for most of the other numbers. Here he was concerned with comparing his beloved with the dearest things he knew, and to Hammerstein this could only involve the wonders of nature and music.

"All the Things You Are" also is an example of the way Hammerstein sweated over every single word in a song. He needed a rhyme for "mine," which was the last word in the lyric, but he could think of nothing else but "divine." The word made sense, and expressed exactly what Hammerstein wanted to say. Nevertheless, through overuse, it had lost its true meaning. It had become trite. Hammerstein labored over the one line for days trying to find a better word, but nothing else seemed as good. "Divine" just had to remain in the lyric despite the lyricist's never-ending displeasure.

Higher and Higher, Rodgers and Hart's only failure since *Jumbo*, was presented in April, 1940. Things went wrong from the start. Originally intended as a star vehicle for dancer Vera Zorina, the show had to be altered to fit singer Marta Eggert when it was discovered that Zorina could not get out of a film contract. This changed the whole style of the musical, and made Rodgers vow that he would never again do a show that required so many drastic changes to fit a new star. The story, incidentally, borrowed liberally from Bernard Shaw's *Pygmalion*, the source of *My Fair Lady*. It was concerned with the way a chambermaid is taught manners and proper English so that she may be passed off as a debutante.

Since *Higher and Higher* was about servants living in a huge mansion, it gave Rodgers and Hart many bright ideas for their songs. They had the servants poke fun at their employers in "Disgustingly Rich," and they used the servants' day off as inspiration for a romantic duet, "Ev'ry Sunday Afternoon and Thursday Night." But the song that revealed the best of Rodgers and Hart was "It Never Entered My Mind." The lyric contained a series of brilliant lines detailing the warnings that a recently jilted young lady had received but had ignored. The rhyming and the images were highly polished and full of unexpected twists. In spite of its humor, however, the song had tragic overtones. This is the basic quality that Rodgers caught so well in his music. It sustained the proper mood of understatement at all times, and it skillfully conveyed the emptiness of the character's life.

Not all the musicals being presented in New York in 1940 were offered on Broadway. The New York World's Fair in

Flushing Meadow had many theatrical entertainments that attracted visitors from all over the world. One of them, a vast outdoor pageant called *American Jubilee*, had book and lyrics by Oscar Hammerstein and music by Arthur Schwartz.

The show offered highlights of important historical events in songs, sketches, and dances. It gave Hammerstein the opportunity to express honest patriotic emotions through actors depicting Revolutionary War soldiers, P. T. Barnum, Abraham Lincoln, Theodore Roosevelt and the crowds at the inauguration of a future President. All this was offered for only a 40-cent admission charge. *American Jubilee* ran from May to October, 1940.

About two months before *American Jubilee* opened and shortly before the opening of *Higher and Higher*, Rodgers received an important letter from John O'Hara, the novelist and short story writer. O'Hara wanted to know whether Rodgers and Hart had read any of his stories about a nightclub entertainer named Joey Evans that had been appearing in *The New Yorker*. He thought that the character and the locale would lend themselves to a musical comedy treatment, and he expressed a desire to work on the show with Rodgers and Hart.

The partners lost no time in making up their minds. They were both well acquainted with the stories and decided within five minutes that they would go ahead with the project right after the opening of *Higher and Higher*. It took no more than a few days after getting O'Hara's letter for the team to sign Gene Kelly and Vivienne Segal to play the leads, and to secure George Abbott as producer-director. All this was achieved before a line of dialogue was written or a song was composed.

Pal Joey opened on December 25, 1940. While admiring the skill of O'Hara's libretto and the score by Rodgers and Hart, audiences seemed divided about the show chiefly because it was about unpleasant people. Certainly, Joey Evans was a far from likable character. He was a conniving nightclub entertainer who was able to get a rich woman to build a nightclub just for him. He never gave a thought to anyone but himself. At the end of the play, after losing both his rich friend and his nightclub, he was still as deceitful as he had been before.

This surely was not the kind of leading man audiences had become accustomed to in the musical theatre. As Rodgers remarked recently, "I think that when *Pal Joey* was done originally, the theatregoing public wasn't ready to meet people like that in a musical comedy. They were all bad except for an innocent young girl who showed a brief interest in Joey. And she was stupid."

Pal Joey was not in favor of bad people. The characters did get their punishments in the end. But it was brave enough to say that such people do exist. It was also brave enough to depict them as human beings instead of cardboard characters. And it was advanced enough to have the musical numbers fill out the personalities and situations with songs that kept close to the story's viewpoint.

We know all about Joey from the dialogue at the beginning of the play. There is never any question that he will lie and cheat to get his way, and this is carried through by the song "I Could Write a Book." Taken by itself, it seems like a perfectly straight love song. But in the scene in which it is sung, it is merely another approach that Joey uses to impress a pretty girl. He has no intention of writing a book. It is just a good line that he thinks the silly girl will swallow.

The most popular song in the score has become "Bewitched, Bothered and Bewildered," though it took a long time for it to catch on. It is a character song sung by the worldly society woman who has fallen for Joey. She has no false ideas about him. She knows that he is nothing more than a "half-pint imitation." But because she likes him, she is willing to overlook his obvious faults. The beautiful construction of the song, of course, is what makes it so durable. Hart's deft rhyming never falters, and Rodgers' musical contributions are no less remarkable. The constant repetition of the main musical theme conveys perfectly the empty, bored life that the lady leads. There is nothing gay in her falling in love. It will merely relieve her dull world for a brief period—just as the line "Bewitched, bothered and bewildered" relieves the main musical theme throughout the song.

Other situations in *Pal Joey* gave Rodgers and Hart an opportunity to burlesque the kind of songs usually heard in cheap nightclub floor shows. This kind of writing was new to Rodgers, and revealed yet another remarkable talent. For a routine requiring the chorus girls to be bathed in a variety of colored lights, the team provided "That Terrific Rainbow," which made fun of such colorful clichés as "red-hot mama," "green with envy," "heart of gold," and others. For another routine in which the girls were dressed as flowers, their song, "In the Flower Garden of My Heart," went through many purposely trite phrases pertaining to gardening. And in "Zip," Rodgers and Hart again showed their knack of combining opposites to achieve a comic effect. Set to a raucous, blaring rhythm, the lyric revealed that stripteaser Gypsy Rose Lee had only intellectual thoughts as she performed her dance.

Pal Joey had a good though not spectacular run the first time it was shown on Broadway. By the time it was revived twelve years later, many things had happened to make audiences accept the story and characters more readily. In particular, it had been the contribution of Rodgers and Hammerstein that had helped pave the way by conditioning audiences to adult themes and well-drawn characters. Yet surely *Pal Joey* was the musical that had first paved the way for the theatre of Rodgers and Hammerstein. "While Joey himself may have

Lorenz Hart and Richard Rodgers in Hollywood in the mid-1930's.

Oscar Hammerstein and composer Jerome Kern during rehearsal of *Music in the Air* (1933). (Vandamm photo.)

Rodgers and Hammerstein early in their partnership.

Newlyweds Alfred Drake and Joan Roberts in the surrey with the fringe on top in *Oklahoma!* (1943). In front are Lee Dixon, Celeste Holm, Joseph Buloff, and Betty Garde. (Vandamm photo.)

Hero Laurence Guittard and heroine Christine Andreas in the 1979 Broadway
production of *Oklahoma!* (Martha Swope photo.)

Jan Clayton and John Raitt in *Carousel* (1945). (Vandamm photo.)

Party scene from *Allegro* (1947), with John Battles and Roberta Jonay in foreground. (Vandamm photo.)

A discussion about *South Pacific* (1949) brings together Joshua Logan, Richard Rodgers, Oscar Hammerstein, Mary Martin, and James Michener. (John Swope photo.)

Ezio Pinza returns to Mary Martin after his dangerous mission in *South Pacific* (1949). The children are Barbara Luna and Michael DeLeon.

Gertrude Lawrence and her son, Sandy Kennedy, arrive in Bangkok in the first scene of *The King and I* (1951). (Vandamm photo.)

Repeating his role in the 1977 Broadway revival of *The King and I*, Yul Brynner gives a royal command to Constance Towers. (Ernst Haas photo.)

The young lovers of *Me and Juliet* (1953), Bill Hayes and Isabel Bigley. (Eileen Darby photo.)

"The Bums' Opera," led by Helen Traubel, in *Pipe Dream* (1955). (Karger-Pix photo.)

Juanita Hall, Miyoshi Umeki and Keye Luke in *Flower Drum Song* (1958). (Friedman-Abeles photo.)

Greeted by the Von Trapp children in *The Sound of Music* (1959) are newly-weds Mary Martin and Theodore Bikel. (Friedman-Abeles photo.)

Julie Andrews in the opening scene of the film version of *The Sound of Music*. (1965).

ROGERS AND HAMMERSTEIN
AROUND THE WORLD

Oklahoma! poster from the Bucharest, Rumania, production. Note that the title has l
exclamation point and that Oscar Hammerstein is uncredited.

The "Honey Bun" scene from the 1955 production of *South Pacific* in Madrid, Spain. Marta Santa-Olalla played Nellie Forbush.

The poster used in Tel Aviv, Israel, to advertise *The King and I* (1966).

Tadao Takashima and Kaoru Yodo had the leading roles when *The Sound of Music* was presented in Tokyo, Japan, in 1965. Note that the number of Von Trapp children, at least for this publicity photo, was increased from seven to twelve.

At a rehearsal of *No Strings* (late in 1961), Rodgers' first musical after the death of Oscar Hammerstein. Gathered around the composer are Richard Kiley, librettist Samuel Taylor, music director Peter Matz, Diahann Carroll, Don Chastain, Bernice Massi, and Mitchell Gregg. (Friedman-Abeles photo.)

been fairly adolescent in his thinking and his morality," Rodgers wrote just before the revival opening, "the show bearing his name certainly wore long pants, and in many respects forced the musical theatre to wear long pants for the first time."

The revival of *Pal Joey* ran for 542 performances on Broadway. Not only was it a longer run than the original production, it was the longest run of any musical comedy by Rodgers and Hart.

Larry Hart did not live to see the great triumph of *Pal Joey* in 1952. By the time he had begun to work on the first production of the play, he was showing signs of extreme illness. His drinking had increased. His disappearances had become longer. His will to work had been almost completely drained. This naturally forced Rodgers to give more and more thought to teaming up with another lyric writer. His relationship with Hart continued to be close, but the problems of working with him were becoming more difficult.

While *Pal Joey* was still playing on Broadway, Rodgers became interested in a new musical being produced and directed by George Abbott. *Best Foot Forward* was to be a brash, youthful show about youngsters at a military school—just the kind of thing that had appealed to Rodgers in *Babes In Arms* and *Too Many Girls*. Here was a chance for him to get away from his day-to-day concern over his partner, and he decided to join Abbott as co-producer. He did not, however, have his name on the program since this would give fuel to talk of a breakup between Rodgers and Hart. Nor did Rodgers have anything to do with the songs. They were created by the bright young team of Hugh Martin and Ralph Blane and included, among others, the rousing "Buckle Down Winsocki."

Early in the fall of 1941, while *Best Foot Forward* was playing in Philadelphia as part of its tryout tour, Rodgers went to visit Oscar Hammerstein. Although they had never worked together professionally, they had always remained good, if not intimate, friends. The previous year, Hammerstein had succumbed to a long-cherished dream. He bought a 200-year-old, 80-acre farm near Doylestown, Pennsylvania. Called Highland Farm, the main house was a large stone and stucco building on a hill overlooking the beautiful rolling Pennsylvania landscape. Oscar and Dorothy Hammerstein could at last become, in the words of the song, "the folks who live on the hill."

Anxious to have his old friend see his new home, Hammerstein invited Rodgers over for a social call. It was during this visit, sandwiched in between the hectic pre-Broadway run of *Best Foot Forward*, that Rodgers first brought up the subject of a possible future collaboration. The composer, of course, was well aware of the lyricist's string of bad luck. But he was sure Hammerstein still had a great talent, one that needed only the right kind of show to be appreciated again. Hammerstein's reaction to the offer was typically selfless. He told Rodgers that he should continue to work with Hart as if nothing were wrong. Then, if Hart were unable to continue, Hammerstein would be glad to finish whatever project they might be doing. However, he added, "I would never think of asking to have my name put on it. I don't even want to discuss any financial consideration."

Nothing more definite was agreed upon. The two men merely agreed to wait and see what would happen.

Hammerstein's *Sunny River*, which opened in December, 1941, was convincing proof that he needed a change just as badly as Rodgers did—though for a different reason. His failure with the modern musical comedy, *Very Warm for May*, plunged him once again into the unreal world of sentimental operetta. And once again his collaborator was Sigmund Romberg. As in *The New Moon*, they chose old New Orleans for their locale, though the period was updated to take in the War of 1812. But there was a heaviness about the plot that even the attractive melodies and lyrics could not obscure. The show lasted 36 performances.

Sunny River was Hammerstein's last musical before he began his partnership with Rodgers. What is remarkable about the team's success is that there was every indication, at least from Hammerstein's record, that it could not succeed. One musical after another had emphasized the librettist's inability to create works for the modern musical theatre. It was only in his collaboration with Jerome Kern that he had contributed librettos and lyrics of genuine substance. For the most part, his career had been too concerned with a form of entertainment that had become dated. By trying to make the musical theatre advance to a near-operatic level, he succeeded only in making it retreat to a form of theatre that he himself—in *Show Boat* and *Music In the Air*—had helped to make obsolete.

In spite of their difficulties, Rodgers and Hart continued on their successful way. Their last original collaboration, *By Jupiter*, had the longest run of any Rodgers and Hart musical produced during Hart's life. But its 427 performances could not exactly be credited solely to the team's book or songs. Opening in June, 1942, it proved to be just the kind of elaborate and slickly professional show that wartime audiences wanted. Its story about the Greek and Amazon war provided three hours of welcome relief from headlines telling of one Allied defeat after another. And in star Ray Bolger it had the most nimble and charming performer on the Broadway stage.

Although none of the songs from *By Jupiter* ever became very popular, they revealed Rodgers and Hart in generally top form. "Wait Till You See Her" was an affecting love song in which the hero tells his friends about the girl he loves rather than telling her directly. In a way, it was a variation on the

Kern-Hammerstein song "I've Told Every Little Star" from *Music In the Air*. Another interesting song from *By Jupiter* was "Nobody's Heart." The theme is a familiar one for Rodgers and Hart, but they gave it an original twist by having their unloved young girl try to talk herself into believing that she doesn't care. Nothing mawkish was allowed to creep into the words or the music. It was a simple, moving expression that was made even more touching by the unexpected "Heigh ho! Who cares?" that comes in immediately after the opening line, "Nobody's heart belongs to me."

By Jupiter was a success, but it had been hard going all the way through. Because of Hart's failing health, most of the songs had to be written in a hospital. Rodgers had even taken a room there and rented a piano just so that he could work near Hart. After their work was finished, Hart was able to leave the hospital but he no longer seemed interested either in the reception of *By Jupiter* or in following it with another show. He was only forty-seven, but his years of wild living had made him look much older. He was thoroughly exhausted from working, and wanted nothing else than to go away for a long rest.

Rodgers had a far different attitude. Once his work on a show was over, his only thought was of his next assignment. The hectic preparations, the cutting, the changing, the last-minute song that had to be written—these are what he always thrived on. Instead of exhausting him, they seemed to give him renewed vitality. Therefore, just as soon as *By Jupiter* opened, all he cared about was a new project, whatever it might be.

He didn't have to wait long.

PART II

THE PARTNERSHIP

CHAPTER 7

Oklahoma!

THE THEATRE GUILD has always been among the great producing organizations in the theatre. In the Twenties, under the
direction of its founders and co-directors, Theresa Helburn
and Lawrence Langner, it had been the first to offer plays by
Eugene O'Neill, Maxwell Anderson, S. N. Behrman, and Sid-
ney Howard. It had introduced the works of Bernard Shaw
to American audiences. By 1942, however, it was going
through a very dark period in its history. One play after another had failed, leaving the once rich Theatre Guild with
very little money in its treasury. Its next production had
to be a success if the Guild was to continue at all.

It was then that Theresa Helburn had an idea. Ever since
Rodgers and Hart had written the songs for the two editions
of *The Garrick Gaieties,* she and Langner had hoped that the
team would someday write the score for another Theatre
Guild musical. They had even once suggested Aristophanes'

Lysistrata as a possibility, but Rodgers thought it was unsuitable.

In 1942, Miss Helburn had in mind a different play, one that the Theatre Guild itself had produced about eleven years before. It was called *Green Grow the Lilacs*. Lynn Riggs' story told a simple folk tale of cowboys and farmers living in that part of the country known as Indian Territory. Although it wasn't a musical, the play made great use of folk songs to lend color to the story. It seemed, in fact, as ready-made for the musical stage as another play once produced by the Theatre Guild, called *Porgy*. If *Porgy*, which had used Negro spirituals, could be turned so successfully into the folk opera *Porgy and Bess*, why couldn't *Green Grow the Lilacs* be turned with equal success into a folk musical?

Almost as soon as Theresa Helburn and Lawrence Langner discussed the idea with Rodgers, he became convinced that this was exactly the kind of show he wanted to do. There was only one problem: Hart was completely uninterested. He didn't think it was their kind of show, he told Rodgers, and besides he wasn't feeling well. He was going to Mexico for a long rest. If Rodgers really wanted to write this new score so badly, he had Hart's permission to find someone else to write the lyrics.

Rodgers then was able to carry out the idea that he had discussed with Hammerstein the previous year. But instead of Hammerstein taking over after Hart quit, the situation now brought Rodgers and Hammerstein together right from the start of the planning. The two men met for lunch and simply agreed to collaborate. Hammerstein even revealed that he had once thought of doing a musical *Green Grow the Lilacs* himself some years before. Enchanted by the play, he had tried to persuade Jerome Kern to write the score with him. The composer, however, thought that the story had too many problems, and turned it down.

Rodgers and Hammerstein worked in harmony right from the start. It was an entirely new experience for Rodgers. Since his only professional collaborator had been Lorenz Hart, he was amazed to find a lyric writer so dependable. With Hart, he usually had to supply the inspiration by composing the music first; with Hammerstein, it was the lyricist who usually wrote first. With Hart, it had been the constant problem of getting him to work; with Hammerstein, it was the comforting experience of knowing where his partner was and that he was always on the job.

The method of collaboration that the men used for *Oklahoma!* set the model for all of their shows. After spending months talking over the story line and the places that they thought required songs, the men would then part. Hammerstein would go to his farm in Pennsylvania, and Rodgers either would go to his apartment in New York or his home in Connecticut.

Hammerstein worked in an office on the second floor of his home. He usually would pace back and forth until an idea came to him. Then he would write it down in longhand at an upright desk that he found comfortable because he hated to keep jumping up all the time. Most of the time he would accompany his lyrics by singing and humming to himself, though his melodies were usually dreadful. Frequently, it took Hammerstein days of concentration to complete the lyric to a song. "A professional toils and sweats and polishes," he once wrote. "He doesn't submit his work to anyone until he has done everything he can think of to make his song good. And then he loves it. He really loves it."

Once Hammerstein felt that he had toiled and sweated and polished enough, he would send it to Rodgers by mail or read him the lines over the telephone. The composer would then promptly get to work and complete the music in a comparatively short while, usually away from the piano. Although

Rodgers always has opposed the notion of inspiration, he does believe that a song is best if the moment of creation is a spontaneous one. However, this outpouring of melody comes only after many long hours of thinking about exactly what kind of song he will write.

Rodgers does not go around with his head full of melodies. He does not just sit down and write a song because he can't get a tune out of his head. He has to have a reason for writing a particular type of song. And that reason is dictated by the play and the character and the situation he is writing for.

All he has ever done, Rodgers insists, is to use notes instead of words or paint or clay to express an emotion. It is an effective medium, he believes, because it can be made to fit any kind of emotion there is. In combination with his partner's lyrics, his music is used to tell his audience exactly what characters in a play are feeling and doing.

The closeness of Rodgers' collaboration with both Hart and with Hammerstein shows how well he has followed his own deep beliefs on the subject. "A good collaboration," he has said, "is one where minds, emotions and intellects meet. Like a good marriage, you have to understand a person's needs. You have to give way to him. It's easier to say, 'Let's try it your way first. Then let's try it my way.' In that way there are no hurt feelings. In all my years of working with Larry Hart and in all my years of working with Oscar Hammerstein, I never had an argument."

No two people were ever more surprised at the great success of *Oklahoma!* than Rodgers and Hammerstein. In fact, they later made up a game about the show. To play the game, they had to believe that *Oklahoma!* had been a flop instead of a hit. Then, like Monday-morning quarterbacks, they proceeded to explain why.

First of all, Rodgers has said, "Everyone connected with the show, except me, had had a string of failures. The Theatre

Guild had made no secret of the fact that this was really their last gasp. This was not very convincing for an investor with money to put in a show. Oscar hadn't had a hit in years. Our choreographer, Agnes de Mille, had withdrawn from two Broadway musicals before they had come to New York. She had staged the dances for an English musical about nine years before, and had done a show in Hoboken. All we really knew about her was that we liked her ballet, *Rodeo*, and we thought she would be right to create the dances. Rouben Mamoulian had had nothing on Broadway since *Porgy and Bess*, and that was in 1935. The cast was completely unknown. Alfred Drake had had a part in *Babes In Arms*, but nobody would go to see a show just because he was in it. Celeste Holm had no previous experience in a musical. Joan Roberts had been on Broadway only once before, in Oscar's *Sunny River*.

"Then what was *Oklahoma!* all about? Cowboys and farmers. Nothing spicy in it. No one was going to be attracted by the costumes. But the main thing that made people sure *Oklahoma!* would fail was that Oscar and I were working together for the first time. Everyone was certain of it because I was writing with a new partner after so many successful years with Larry."

"As far as the show was concerned," Hammerstein liked to point out, "one would wonder how two professionals could make so many mistakes. The chorus girls did not appear until the curtain had been up for about forty minutes. One of our best songs, 'Oh, What a Beautiful Mornin',' was wasted in the first three minutes of the play while the audience was still being seated. As for the story, the first act is about a girl trying to make up her mind which man, Curly or Jud, will take her to a dance. There is almost no other plot. In the second act, no important new numbers were introduced, except for the song 'Oklahoma!' This show just had to fail."

Rodgers and Hammerstein did not play this little game just

to gloat. Their point was to show that it is impossible to draw
up any kind of a formula that will guarantee success, or to set
up rules about what they should or should not do. *Oklahoma!*
did not become such a towering success merely because it was
different. It succeeded because of the skills that went into it.
True, the production staff, except for Rodgers, had not enjoyed success in many years. True, the cast was largely un-
tried. True, a warmhearted tale of cowboys and farmers was
not the usual fare being offered on Broadway. But what was
also true was that the show was being assembled by talented
people with deep convictions. They believed firmly in what
they were doing. They did not say, "Look how different and
clever we are" or "Aren't we brave to do things no one ever
tried before?" What they did say was "This has never been
done before, but it works and we like it. Why shouldn't we
do it?"

When Rodgers, Hammerstein, Mamoulian, and Miss de
Mille got together for the first time, they decided right from
the start that there would have to be an over-all plan for the
entire production. No one would sing a song, do a bit of business, or leap into the air with the idea of stopping the show.
Everything would have to have a purpose, everything would
be in character, everything would fit into the story.

The authors were determined that they wouldn't open the
musical with a barn dance or a quilting party. That would
have been too obvious. Therefore, after talking things over
carefully, they came to the conclusion that the best way to
open *Oklahoma!* was to do it in the same way that Lynn Riggs
had opened *Green Grow the Lilacs*. That is, with a woman
seated alone on the stage churning butter. And the song "Oh,
What a Beautiful Mornin' " was then used by the cowboy
hero, Curly McLain, to put into words and music what Riggs
had described in his original stage directions: "It is a radiant
summer morning several years ago, the kind of morning

which, enveloping the shapes of earth—men, cattle in a meadow, blades of the young corn, streams—makes them seem to exist now for the first time, their images giving off a visible golden emanation that is partly true and partly a trick of imagination focusing to keep alive a loveliness that may pass away . . ."

Here was a perfect idea for a song to set the mood for the entire show. To put in the song all the peace and contentment of a sun-drenched day on a farm, Rodgers used a lazy waltz rhythm, and Hammerstein created a perfect poetic description of such a day. From Riggs' lines about cattle, corn, and the "visible golden emanation," Hammerstein took his ideas about cattle standing like statues, the reference to the height of the corn, and the sight of the bright golden haze on the meadow. To these he added his own feelings, including a reference to music in the line "All the sounds of the earth are like music."

The line "The corn is as high as an elephant's eye" was originally written "The corn is as high as a cow pony's eye." But this didn't please Hammerstein for two reasons. First, he found that corn actually grows higher than a cow pony's eye. Second, and most important, even though "cow pony's eye" was suited to the Western locale, the words would be hard to understand when heard for the first time. "Elephant's eye" was not only a more accurate height, but it sounded better. In fact, when Rodgers first saw the lyric to the song, he was so moved that, as he later recalled, "I was a little sick with joy because it was so lovely and so right. When you're given words like 'The corn is as high as an elephant's eye,' you've got something to say musically." This was the first professional song they wrote together.

The other songs in *Oklahoma!* fit into place with equally good effect. "People Will Say We're In Love" is a roundabout way in which the two lovers, Laurey and Curly, are able to convey their love while still in the midst of a lovers' quarrel. Even though a love song was needed in this particular situation, they couldn't possibly admit that they were in love. Therefore, what they do is merely warn each other against showing affection so that neighbors won't get the wrong (or right) idea.

Probably the song that affected Hammerstein the most deeply was "The Surrey With the Fringe On Top." With its catchy clip-clop beat imitating hoofbeats and its delight in simple pleasures, it is a song that could always make the lyricist weep no matter how often he heard it. "I think of two people who are looking forward that much to a ride in a surrey," he once said. "I guess it's a kind of assurance of faith in people's over-all goodness. I've met a couple of villains in my life, but most people are trying so hard—sometimes they fail, but they try—to be good to one another."

Oklahoma! was not all goodness. The villainous character, Jud Fry, was, as Hammerstein put it, "the bass fiddle to give body to the orchestration of the story." But how to keep him from becoming too much of a villain was the big problem. This was solved by two songs, "Pore Jud" and "Lonely Room." In "Pore Jud," he is revealed as a somewhat comic and pathetic figure, dreaming of the tears being shed over him at his funeral. In "Lonely Room," he sings of his unhappy, lonely life. Jud Fry may not have been someone you'd want to meet, but at least Rodgers and Hammerstein made him understandable.

The big, rousing title song was saved until the end of the play. Rodgers' music was so charged that audiences could almost feel the wind come sweeping down the plain. The number is another expression of Hammerstein's talent for painting his idealized life surrounded by the beauties of nature. For whether it be in Egern by the Tegern See, or in a farmhouse on top of a hill, or in the soon-to-become state of Oklahoma, to Hammerstein there was nothing more soul-satisfying than looking out across calm, contented waters, or having a veranda with a view of meadows green, or watching a hawk making lazy circles in the sky.

During the pre-Broadway tryout of *Oklahoma!* in New Haven and Boston, the reports about the show were good, but no one really expected it to become the biggest hit in the history of the musical theatre. One newspaper writer even telegraphed his editor: NO GALS NO GAGS NO CHANCE.

Nobody liked the original title, *Away We Go!*, and many different ones were suggested. These included *Swing Your Lady*, *Cherokee Strip*, and *Yes-sirree*. But when Boston audiences became so excited about the song "Oklahoma," it was decided to use that name as the play's new title. The exclamation point was then added to prevent people from confusing the musical with a story about John Steinbeck's Okies, the name given to the migratory workers in his novel, *The Grapes of Wrath*.

The New York opening of *Oklahoma!* took place on March 31, 1943. The show had a small advance sale, and not all the seats had been sold for the first performance. But the enthusiasm of the audiences quickly spread, and it lasted five years and nine weeks on Broadway. Its national touring company was on the road for ten and a half years, playing in 153 cities in the United States and ten in Canada. It has also been performed throughout the world.

One reason for the success of *Oklahoma!* that should not be overlooked was that it gave wartime audiences a chance to feel pride in an important page of our country's history. It implied a hopefulness about the future, while still letting people enjoy the pleasures of a simpler, sunnier period of the past.

CHAPTER 8

Temporary Separation and
State Fair

I N SPITE OF THE huge success of *Oklahoma!*, Rodgers and
Hammerstein had not yet become a permanent team. There
was still no final break between Rodgers and Hart, and it was
expected that they would resume their partnership once *Oklahoma!* was completed.

There was no question that Larry Hart admired what
Rodgers had achieved in *Oklahoma!* But his feeling of inse-
curity was certainly not helped by Rodgers' scoring such a hit
the first time he wrote with another partner. Aware of this,
Rodgers thought of a way to get Hart back to work again.
Rodgers would produce an updated version of *A Connecticut
Yankee*, the great Rodgers and Hart musical of the Twenties.
Since it would require only a few new songs, the production
would not tax Hart's failing health too much. But more impor-
tant, it would give Hart a much-needed boost to his morale.

With the original librettist, Herbert Fields, writing the revised story, the celebrated trio of Rodgers, Hart and Fields was reunited for the last time.

In order to make the sixteen-year-old *A Connecticut Yankee* fit into the wartime world of 1943, Fields turned his hero into a naval officer, and even had him introduce the jeep to the knights of King Arthur's Camelot. He also enlarged the minor part of the wicked Queen Morgan Le Fay to fit the major talents of Vivienne Segal.

Rodgers and Hart worked well together. Hart stuck to the job with renewed interest, chiefly because he wanted to prove that he was still a master at writing lyrics. There was surely no doubt about it, particularly with his words to the song "To Keep My Love Alive." Set to a dainty, folk-type melody, the piece listed in deadpan innocence a gory résumé of all the husbands Queen Morgan Le Fay had put to death. The charm of the music, the brilliance of the rhyming, and the perfect way it was sung by Miss Segal all added up to one of the most hilarious numbers Rodgers and Hart had ever written.

But Larry Hart was never able to enjoy its success. Emotionally worn out even by his limited work for the new production, he disappeared during the opening-night performance of *A Connecticut Yankee*. He was found a few days later sprawled across his hotel room bed, running a high fever. Rodgers had him rushed to Doctors Hospital. Three days later, at the age of forty-eight, he died of pneumonia.

Even if Larry Hart had lived, it is unlikely that he would have continued to write with Rodgers. In a sense, their partnership had ended the day Theresa Helburn telephoned Rodgers to ask if he might be interested in writing a musical about farmers and cowmen.

Within his tragically short life, however, Hart produced lyrics that still are regarded as among the most brilliant ever created for popular songs. He was both pioneer and prophet in making the once trite song lyric into a thing of beauty, wit, and meaning. His tragedy was that he had to destroy himself in order to create.

Practically speaking, the death of Lorenz Hart freed Rodgers completely to work with Hammerstein. However, Hammerstein, too, had a project of his own. At the same time Rodgers was preparing *A Connecticut Yankee*, his new partner was working on something even more ambitious. This was his modern version of the opera *Carmen*, called *Carmen Jones*.

Carmen Jones, which opened just two weeks after *A Connecticut Yankee*, took only minor liberties with the music of composer Georges Bizet and with the outline of the opera's plot. The basic change was in turning the soldiers and workers of southern Spain into American Negro soldiers and workers in the Southern United States. But so carefully were the changes made that the new version never became just a stunt. It was a work that could be accepted on its own merit. The music filled out the colorful story and was equally right for the new locale. Hammerstein's lyrics showed his customary skill at expressing the emotions of ordinary people. They not only fitted the familiar arias, duets, and choruses, but actually sounded as if both lyricist and composer had worked in closest harmony.

Perhaps what was most significant about *Carmen Jones* was that it proved *Oklahoma!* was no accident. After more than twenty years, Oscar Hammerstein, 2nd, was at last recognized as the outstanding lyricist-librettist in the theatre. He was no longer overshadowed by the reputation of his collaborator, whether it was a Kern or a Friml or a Romberg. The team of Rodgers and Hammerstein—like the team of Rodgers and Hart—was an equal partnership. Even so celebrated a composer as Georges Bizet did not have his name on the program of *Carmen Jones* in larger letters than Oscar Hammerstein's.

In addition, *Oklahoma!* and *Carmen Jones* also showed that

Hammerstein no longer needed to rely on operetta as a means of breaking away from ordinary musical comedy. Like *Show Boat, Rainbow,* and *Music In the Air,* these were true examples of musical plays. That is, the characters and the situations were human and believable. They had successfully bridged the gap between musical comedy on one side and operetta on the other. And they had pointed the way in which Rodgers and Hammerstein were to move most successfully in their later productions.

Yet the acclaim of these two musicals within one year did not change Oscar Hammerstein. He had won acclaim before, but he had had too much experience in the theatre not to expect the future to have disappointments as well as successes. Modestly, he placed a full-page advertisement (see page 114) in the anniversary issue of *Variety,* the theatrical trade newspaper, listing five Hammerstein plays that had had short runs.

This show of modesty turned out to be more of a reminder of what *could* happen than what *would* happen in Hammerstein's subsequent career. No stage musical by Rodgers and Hammerstein ever had a run of under thirty weeks.

The team was also successful in the one film they worked on. In 1933, the Fox Film Corporation had made a movie version of Phil Stong's novel, *State Fair.* A little over ten years later, the studio (now known as 20th Century-Fox) decided to produce a second screen version. This time, however, they wanted to do it as a musical. The rustic charm of *Oklahoma!* immediately suggested to the studio heads that Rodgers and Hammerstein would be just right at creating songs that would capture the equally rustic charm of an Iowa state fair.

When they were asked, Rodgers and Hammerstein liked the idea immediately. However, it was impossible for them to leave New York at that time. The team had just become busi-

Holiday Greetings

OSCAR HAMMERSTEIN, II

author of

Sunny River

(Six Weeks at the St. James Theatre, New York)

Very Warm For May

(Seven Weeks at the Alvin Theatre, New York)

Three Sisters

(Six Weeks at the Drury Lane, London)

Ball at the Savoy

(Five Weeks at the Drury Lane, London)

Free For All

(Three Weeks at the Manhattan Theatre, New York)

★ ★ ★ ★ ★ ★ ★

I'VE DONE IT BEFORE AND
I CAN DO IT AGAIN

ness partners as well as writing partners, and they could not spare the time to move to California to work on the film.

The first business step was to form their own music publishing firm, which they named Williamson Music, Inc., because both Rodgers and Hammerstein were sons of men named William. Soon they branched out to become theatrical producers of plays by other writers. These were *I Remember Mama* by John van Druten, *Happy Birthday* by Anita Loos, *John Loves Mary* by Norman Krasna, *The Happy Time* by Samuel Taylor, *The Heart of the Matter* by Graham Greene, and *Burning Bright* by John Steinbeck. All but the last two were successful. Rodgers and Hammerstein also produced two musicals that they did not collaborate on: *Annie Get Your Gun* with a book by Herbert and Dorothy Fields and a score by Irving Berlin, and a touring production of Kern and Hammerstein's *Show Boat*.

It was during the hectic months of organizing their company that Rodgers wrote the music and Hammerstein wrote the screenplay and lyrics for the film remake of *State Fair*. In all, they wrote seven songs, though one number, "We Will Be Together," was dropped before the movie was released.

The close fusion of words and music that distinguished the best works of Rodgers and Hammerstein is especially apparent in the score for *State Fair*. One song was needed at the beginning of the film to establish the fact that a young girl has all the symptoms of spring fever. Hammerstein worked over the idea until he realized with a shock that state fairs are held only in the fall. Then he got an even better idea. Even though it was autumn, the girl would feel *as if* it were spring. Still a bit unsure of himself, Hammerstein talked over the idea with Rodgers, who thought it would be great. The composer was even more excited when he saw the finished lyric with its appropriate image of the girl feeling as restless as a willow in a windstorm and as jumpy as a puppet on a string. Lines such as these, Rodgers has said, actually provided him with an almost inevitable musical pathway. They gave him the form on which he could compose a melody that would be, in his words, "feminine, young, nervous, and, if possible, pretty like the girl." The music has the quality of restlessness and of jumpiness indicated in the lyric, and since the girl is uncertain of her own feeling, the line "jumpy as a puppet on a string" ends on the musical note of F-natural, which gives it a slightly uncertain quality.

If the heroine could compare herself to a nightingale without a song to sing in "It Might as Well Be Spring," a whole group of fairgoers revealed a different emotion as they described a bird throwing its heart to the sky in "It's a Grand Night for Singing." Set to a swooping melody that almost defies a listener to keep from joining in, the lyric goes directly to the things that give people the urge to sing—a warm, moonlit, starry night and the sudden thrill of falling in love.

The sweet and simple flavor of *State Fair* helped to turn it into the movie's answer to *Oklahoma!* The story and setting, of course, were entirely different, but the film conveyed the general contentment of country living and the pleasures to be found in such simple things in life as winning blue ribbons at a state fair.

CHAPTER 9

Carousel

Bᴇᴄᴀᴜsᴇ sʜᴇ ʜᴀᴅ been instrumental in bringing Rodgers and Hammerstein together, Theresa Helburn was constantly on the lookout for new story ideas that might interest the partners. Naturally, her first thought was of plays that had been produced by the Theatre Guild, and she read through dozens of them as part of her quest. The one she decided on was Ferenc Molnar's *Liliom*, which the Guild had produced in 1921.

This would be quite a change from *Oklahoma! Liliom* was a major play by a major European playwright. It was a fantasy about a shiftless carnival barker in Budapest who marries a shy young factory worker. He kills himself in a holdup attempt in order to avoid capture by the police. When taken to Heaven, he refuses to express sorrow for his action, and is sent to Hell. After sixteen years there, he is allowed to return to earth for one day to atone for his sins. Dressed as a beggar, he tries to give his daughter a star he has stolen, but she refuses to take it. He slaps her and is led away.

As soon as she had made up her mind that this was the perfect play for Rodgers and Hammerstein to turn into a musical, Miss Helburn invited the team to lunch to talk the matter over. But when she got through explaining what a wonderful musical could be made out of *Liliom*, the partners shook their heads. How in the world could this be made into a musical? What about the unsympathetic leading character? What about his death midway through the second act? What about the unfamiliar European locale? What about the gloomy ending? No, no, Rodgers and Hammerstein told her, this never could work out.

But Theresa Helburn was persistent, and Rodgers and Hammerstein agreed to give it further thought. The following week they met at Hammerstein's house. If you don't like the Budapest locale, Miss Helburn suggested to the partners, why not move it to New Orleans? That would put it in the United States, but it could still retain a European flavor. Liliom could be a Creole. This, however, was ruled out when Hammerstein protested his unfamiliarity with the dialect.

What about the New England coast, then? suggested Rodgers. This was more logical. The ensemble could consist of sailors, fishermen, and girls who worked in the mills. The amusement park where the barker works could be located on the seaboard. More than that, Hammerstein felt that the people themselves, "people who were strong and alive and lusty, people who had always been shown on the stage as thin-lipped Puritans," would give the play a great deal of vitality. This was particularly true of Julie, the leading female character, whose inner strength and outer simplicity seemed to him closer to New England than to Budapest. And Liliom, the strutting carnival barker, was a character who could fit any surroundings.

Thus, doubts gave way to enthusiasm as the whole structure of the musical *Liliom* began to take shape in the minds of Rodgers and Hammerstein. But there was still one major stumbling block: What to do about the play's basic pessimism? Molnar's ending, with Liliom's daughter left helpless and hopeless, was impossible for Rodgers and Hammerstein to accept. There had to be a lesson that the girl learns from her father.

The way Rodgers and Hammerstein solved the problem in *Carousel* was both theatrically effective and fitting to the story. Their final scene was the graduation exercises of the local school. In a speech, the town doctor advises the boys and girls in the class to stand on their own two feet, because with faith and courage they'll come out all right. This reminds him of a song he used to sing in school, "You'll Never Walk Alone," and all the students, except for Louise, the daughter, join in. Her father, who has returned to earth from pugatory, pleads with her to listen to the words. Although he is unseen by anyone, he manages to communicate with the girl. Somewhat tentatively, she joins in the singing, and a classmate puts her arm around her shoulder. The girl now has hope in her heart. She will never walk alone.

This need for faith is a very important part of the philosophy of Rodgers and Hammerstein. It is not necessarily a religious faith, but a faith that people should have in themselves and in each other. Thus in *Carousel* there is the first glimmer of the spirit of brotherhood that is contained in most of the later musical plays of Rodgers and Hammerstein. It is this feeling that led Hammerstein to become interested in the movement for World Federalism, which calls for a supergovernment that all countries would obey. In a small scale, that is what he and Rodgers were trying to say in *Carousel*. No man is an island, people need people, without understanding there is no meaning to life. The young girl in the play can only find happiness by becoming friendly toward others.

With the major problems of adaptation ironed out, Rodgers and Hammerstein were once again associated with the Theatre Guild. Their production staff, led by director Rouben Mamoulian and choreographer Agnes de Mille, was almost the same as the one for *Oklahoma!* Even their leading man, John Raitt, had played Curly in the Chicago company of *Oklahoma!* Opening in April, 1945, *Carousel* ran over two years on Broadway and then toured for another two years.

Of all his works, Rodgers has always considered *Carousel* to be his finest score. It is not hard to see why.

From the outset, Rodgers and Hammerstein were determined to make *Carousel* a musical play *based* on *Liliom*, not *Liliom* with some additional songs. It had to have its own style and not depend on people's familiarity with the original. Yet it would also have to be faithful to the general spirit of the Molnar play. In the first meeting between Billy Bigelow (the new name for Liliom) and Julie, they talk about the same sort of things that the original characters did. Yet here the music heightens the drama, and probes deeper into the characters than the straight dialogue was able to. For example, the original play contains this brief, stammering exchange:

> LILIOM: But you wouldn't dare to marry anyone like me, would you?
> JULIE: I know that—that—if I loved anyone—it wouldn't make any difference to me what he—even if I died for it.
> LILIOM: But you wouldn't marry a rough guy like me—that is—eh—if you loved me—
> JULIE: Yes, I would—if I loved you, Mr. Liliom.

In *Carousel*, Rodgers and Hammerstein expanded the sentiment into an eloquent song, "If I Loved You," dealing with the awkward way Julie and Billy would behave if they were in love. First Julie sings of how absent-minded she would be, and that she would be too afraid and shy to express her true feelings. Then Billy sings how awful he would feel. The two people never admit they are in love, but the music and lyric involves the audience in the couple's emotions. There is no doubt of the depth of their feelings.

The musical continued Rodgers and Hammerstein's pioneering work in stagecraft. Because of the almost operatic theme of the play, the orchestra used more instruments than had ever been used before for a Broadway musical. *Carousel* had no overture. Instead, the expressive "Carousel Waltz" was played to set the scene of the carnival, with characters performing in pantomime.

The integration between dialogue and song was smoothly done. In an early scene, Julie and her friend, Carrie Pipperidge, are seated on a park bench talking about "beaux." At first the music is used merely as background to their conversation. Then, with the audience hardly aware of it, they are soon conversing in song. The duet "You're a Queer One, Julie Jordan" emerges naturally as a conversation set to music. It then leads into the solo in which Carrie admits her love for a fish-smelling, pompous fisherman named Mr. Snow. Here again, in spite of the song's humor, Hammerstein has made it a very tender expression by having Carrie imagine the church wedding and what it will be like to go home to their cottage by the sea.

As they had done with "Oh, What a Beautiful Mornin'," Rodgers and Hammerstein used "June Is Bustin' Out All Over" to show the influence of weather. But while the song from *Oklahoma!* had a lazy, self-satisfied air, the song from *Carousel* is a bright, frisky expression that describes the crazy ways usually normal people react to the first signs of summer.

In *Oklahoma!* Rodgers and Hammerstein had used two songs to help audiences understand the villainous Jud Fry. For *Carousel* they had the even more difficult job of creating a song to help explain their not very attractive "hero," Billy

Bigelow. Billy has never done anything worthwhile in his life, but he must have the audience's sympathy as well as understanding. What was needed was a song to reveal his rather mixed-up character, something that would show both his good intentions and also his inability to live up to them. Rodgers and Hammerstein decided to put such a song into the scene in which Billy first learns that he is to become a father.

The song was called "Soliloquy." At the beginning of the piece, the father-to-be imagines his child-to-be as a boy. He is full of pride as he dreams of how he and his son Bill will have fun together. The music matches the words, with one note striding forcefully after another. But then Billy interrupts himself. Suppose Julie doesn't have a boy. Suppose it's a girl. Suddenly, he realizes how little he has to give her. He'll have to be a real father to a girl, and he's not sure he knows how. Now, with the music mirroring his changed mood, he becomes wistful about his girl, describing how delicate she will be and how she will be wooed by the local lads. But again he interrupts his reverie. His little girl will grow hungry if he continues his shiftless life. With tension mounting in both words and music, he vows that he will do anything to get enough money to bring up his daughter properly. He will make it or steal it or take it—or die.

That lyric, which occupies four pages of the play's printed text, took Hammerstein two solid weeks to write. When he handed it to Rodgers, the composer promptly went to work and turned out the music in less than two hours.

The speed with which Rodgers works has become one of the legends of the theatre. Yet it is not accurate to say that he merely dashes off tune after tune. For he and Hammerstein had already spent days in talking about a song before he put one note on paper—what it would be about, who would sing it, how it would fit the action. Therefore, when Hammerstein gave him the words to "Soliloquy," Rodgers had been thinking about the song for a long time. He knew just what kind of music he was going to write. As he once explained, "When I get an idea for a song, I can hear it in the orchestra. I can smell it in the scenery. I can see the kind of actor who'll sing the song and the audience there listening to it. Even before I wrote 'Soliloquy,' I had said to Oscar, 'How would this be for a song?' And I told him about it. Not the actual notes in the music, but the color of it and the thought. And he saw what I saw in it."

If "Soliloquy" is the perfect expression of the character of Billy Bigelow, the song "What's the Use of Wond'rin'?" is the perfect expression of Julie's character. It is impossible for Julie not to love Billy. As she reveals, she is his girl and he is her feller and all the rest is talk. It is a simple statement of fact, mated to a simple yet compelling melody. Nevertheless, Hammerstein admitted having trouble with the lyric, especially that final word "talk" with its hard "k" sound. Most songs end with an open vowel or a weak consonent, so that the singer can frequently hold the final note as long as his lungs hold out. But a singer could not hold the final note of "What's the Use of Wond'rin'?" very long because the "k" sound would cut it short. Although he was well aware of this, Hammerstein used the word because it said exactly what he wanted the girl to say. Afterwards, however, he always felt that the song would have had wider appeal if, instead of "and all the rest is talk," he had ended the piece with "that's all you have to know."

Carousel made it two stage successes in a row for Rodgers and Hammerstein. They had gone from the open-air charm of the American Midwest to a bittersweet fantasy with equal distinction. In fact, it was easy for theatregoers to have their choice of either play. For about two years, *Carousel* at the Majestic Theatre and *Oklahoma!* at the St. James faced each other across West 44th Street, in New York.

CHAPTER 10

Allegro

THE FIRM OF Rodgers and Hammerstein was now in full
swing. It seemed that everything the partners touched could
not help but become a success. But success did not make them
want to take things easy. They were constantly talking over
new and exciting ideas. Adapting other people's works and
producing other people's plays had given them great satisfaction. But they felt that the time had come for them to write
something entirely original, something that would not depend
on someone else's play or book. Therefore, they began to talk
over an original idea for a musical that would express the personal philosophy of Rodgers and Hammerstein. The musical
eventually became *Allegro*.

Writing an original musical play presents many difficult
problems. Since a musical is a bringing together of all theatrical
arts—story, song, dance, costumes, scenery, lighting—it requires the greatest care in all departments to make the result
come out smoothly. With such a variety of ingredients, it is

little wonder that most of our great works in the field have relied on plays and books that have already gained popularity. It gives everyone a head start to work with familiar characters and situations. Shakespeare, of course, borrowed many well-known plots for his plays, and most of the grand operas are based on previously accepted works.

Nevertheless, most writers for the musical theatre dream of doing something entirely original. Rodgers and Hammerstein were no exception. Besides, *Allegro* would be a special kind of a musical, one that was almost epic in concept. It would tell the story of the first 35 years in the life of a young doctor. Its theme would be the difficulties a man has in keeping his integrity in the modern world. And it would be presented without conventional scenery, and with a Greek chorus to comment on the action and characters.

Allegro opened on Broadway in October, 1947, under the sponsorship of the Theatre Guild. Though it never achieved the popularity of some of the other Rodgers and Hammerstein plays, it was always one of their special favorites. Unlike the game they played with *Oklahoma!*, the team never had to imagine that the show was not a success. They were always honest about its relative failure. "I wanted to write a large, universal story," Hammerstein once said, "and I think I overestimated the ability of the audience to identify itself with the leading character." Realizing the difficulty that the play had in getting its theme across, Hammerstein frequently talked about rewriting it, but he was never able to find time to do it.

Rodgers and Hammerstein had been concerned about the basic theme of *Allegro* for a long time. They were disturbed about what Hammerstein once referred to as the conspiracy that takes place after a man is successful to keep him from what he is supposed to be doing. If he is a successful doctor, he suddenly finds himself running a hospital instead of directly caring for the sick. If he is a writer or a lawyer, he finds himself on committees or running corporations instead of trying to create great works of literature or defending people in trouble.

What most upset Rodgers and Hammerstein was that many people thought they were merely concerned with praising poor country doctors at the expense of rich city doctors. The play's hero does return to his small town after giving up his chance for promotion in a big Chicago hospital, but this was not the point. There was even a line in the play explaining that it was not a conflict between city doctors and country doctors. In one scene, Joe Taylor, the leading character, says, "There's nothing wrong with people just because they have money or live in the city—nothing wrong with being a city doctor."

However, despite the very real problem of integrity that was the main theme of *Allegro*, Hammerstein could not completely hide his preference for country living. In the important final song, "Come Home," the disillusioned doctor is lured back to his hometown by the description of a bird flying to a tall green tree as "no finer sight for a man to see," and the sound of breezes singing by a laughing spring as "no sweeter sound for a man to hear."

Because Rodgers' father had been a doctor, some people identified the composer with the main character. It was actually Hammerstein, however, who put a great deal of himself into the part of Joe Taylor. Like Hammerstein, the hero in *Allegro* learns of death at an early age when his grandmother dies. His mother dies when he is about the same age as Hammerstein had been when *his* mother had died, and his attitudes toward his work and his school were taken from the author's own experiences.

Allegro also gave Rodgers and Hammerstein the opportunity to write in a satirical vein which had not been apparent in their previous scores. Even before our earnest young doctor goes to the big city there is a mocking quartet of housewives poking fun at the philosophy that "Money Isn't Everything" ("As long as you have dough"). Our first glimpse of Chicago is at a fashionable cocktail party at which the dull conversation is conveyed through the gibberish of "Yatata Yatata Yatata." Later, the mood gets even more bitter as the title song uses the musical term to describe the frantic pace of modern city living. Hammerstein even indulged in a sophisticated torch song, "The Gentleman Is a Dope," which expresses the feelings of a too-bright girl in love with her not-so-bright boss.

But *Allegro* also reveals the more firmly held Rodgers and Hammerstein attitudes. The simple and direct "A Fellow Needs a Girl" shows the happy partnership of man and wife sharing the pleasures and the problems of the day. Also, to the rushing tempo of "You Are Never Away," the girl is compared with a song, a rainbow, a morning in spring, and the star in the lace of a wild willow tree.

In order to make all the elements of *Allegro* blend smoothly, Rodgers and Hammerstein called in Agnes de Mille, who had choreographed *Oklahoma!* and *Carousel,* to direct the entire production. Though having a dance director stage a musical was still unusual at that time, it has now become standard practice in the theatre. Miss de Mille's work was especially difficult since not only did song, dance, and story have to be integrated, but there was also the innovation of the Greek chorus. On stage during most of the play, it set the action, explained characters, talked to the characters, and tried to make everyone in the audience feel as if he were the play's central character.

Allegro was also daring in its settings. Jo Mielziner took care of the problem of swiftly moving scenes by using different stage levels and backdrops, and by his imaginative use of lighting.

Perhaps *Allegro* was ahead of its time. Nevertheless, it ran 315 performances in New York before touring for six and a half months. Perhaps someday, someone will revise it and give it a new chance. Its composer has never lost faith in it. "The comments we made on the compromises demanded by success," Rodgers maintains, "as well as some of the satiric side issues—hypochondria, the empty cocktail party—still hold."

CHAPTER 11

South Pacific

ONE THING was certain. No matter what its virtues may have been, *Allegro* was considered a setback for Rodgers and Hammerstein. This did not make them very happy, but neither did it make them feel like quitting. And it certainly did not make them cautious. It would have been understandable if they were next to turn to something a little less daring, a little less controversial. But this never occurred to them. They firmly believed that they had only themselves to blame if the viewpoint of *Allegro* had failed to be understood by the public. This didn't mean that they should never again do a play like *Allegro*. It only meant that they would have to be extremely careful in the future to make their meanings so clear that they could not be misunderstood.

Rodgers and Hammerstein had brought the musical theatre to a new artistic level. There could be no turning back. *Allegro* had important things to say about man's relationship to society. And with their next play, *South Pacific*, the authors enlarged their outlook to take in the even more challenging theme of man's relationship to man.

The team became involved with *South Pacific* in a round-about way. The first person to see the dramatic possibilities in James Michener's book, *Tales of the South Pacific*, was Kenneth MacKenna, then the head of the story department of Metro-Goldwyn-Mayer. Naturally, he first thought of the work for the screen. After a number of conferences, however, he decided that it might not be right for the films after all, though he still thought it should be dramatized. One evening, MacKenna had dinner with his brother, Jo Mielziner, the stage designer (MacKenna had taken their mother's maiden name), and Joshua Logan, the playwright and director. During the meal, MacKenna recommended the book to Logan, who lost no time reading it. Logan saw the stage possibilities at once. Soon he had joined with Leland Hayward to produce it as a play.

After much discussion, the two men began to realize that *Tales of the South Pacific* would be even more ideal as a musical. A short while later, Logan met Rodgers at a cocktail party. They were old friends, dating back about ten years to Rodgers and Hart's *I Married an Angel*, which Logan had directed. More recently, he had directed the hugely successful *Annie Get Your Gun*, which Rodgers and Hammerstein had produced. Naturally, the talk got around to what shows each would be doing next. Rodgers confessed that while he and Hammerstein were anxious to get started on a new musical, they just had not found anything to interest them. Did Logan have any suggestions? Logan fairly shouted at him that he certainly did have a suggestion, and what's more it was something the three of them could do together. Rodgers promptly took out his notebook and scrawled *T. of the S.P.* in it. But Logan never did hear from him about it.

A few weeks later, Hammerstein had occasion to telephone

Logan, and he casually asked him if he had any ideas for a new musical. Logan, somewhat taken aback, asked lamely if Rodgers hadn't spoken to him about *T. of the S.P.* No, Hammerstein replied, but he'd get the book as soon as possible. The next morning, full of excitement, he called Rodgers. Had Rodgers read *Tales of the South Pacific*, and what did he think of it as the basis for a musical? "Yes, I read it," replied Rodgers. "It's wonderful. Ideal. But a few weeks ago I met someone at a party who owns it and we can't have it."

Thus by forgetting who had told him about the book and the reason Logan had brought up the matter, Rodgers had almost let *South Pacific* slip through his—and Hammerstein's—fingers. It wasn't long before they were committed to write the musical. They also joined Logan and Hayward as co-producers.

As with all of their productions, Rodgers and Hammerstein spent many days in talking over the shape that *South Pacific* would assume on the stage. Four months were spent just talking before a note of music or a line of dialogue was written. And, as usual, there would be special problems. Since the locale of the book was an island during World War II, there would have to be particular care given to the way music was to be integrated with the realistic South Pacific setting. For that reason, it was also decided that formal choreography would be completely out of place.

Because *Tales of the South Pacific* was composed of short stories dealing with various incidents during the war, it was difficult to decide which one to use. Logan particularly liked the story called "Fo' Dollah," which dealt with the unhappy love affair between Joe Cable, a naval lieutenant, and Liat, a native girl. But after trying to approach it from many different angles, the writers felt that the story was too close to that of Puccini's opera, *Madama Butterfly*. They soon hit upon another tale that seemed more logical. It was called "Our

Heroine," and it told of a bright young Navy nurse from Little Rock named Nellie Forbush and her romance with a middle-aged French planter, Emile de Becque. At last the pieces seemed to fall into place, particularly since they found that they could still use the "Fo' Dollah" tale as a secondary plot. The two stories could then be brought together by having Cable join de Becque on a mission behind Japanese lines.

The outline of the plot of *South Pacific* was all set and work was started putting the musical into shape. But with rehearsals already scheduled, Hammerstein had not yet completed the script. Somehow he could not make the dialogue of the sailors ring true. Logan's previous experience in the Navy was what was needed, and he was delighted to accept Hammerstein's invitation to collaborate on the libretto. They finished the job in a month.

While the story and the songs were still being decided on, Rodgers and Hammerstein began to worry about the leads. They knew that their French planter would have to be someone who could not only act but sing. Then they heard a rumor that seemed too good to be true. Ezio Pinza, for years one of the greatest bassos in the Metropolitan Opera Company, was anxious to appear in a Broadway musical. The partners were sure that he would make the perfect Emile de Becque, and they soon signed him to a contract. Their Nellie was found in Mary Martin, who had just completed touring in the national company of *Annie Get Your Gun*. Now, for the first time in their joint careers, Rodgers and Hammerstein had two well-known stars in the leading roles of one of their musicals.

Even before the New York opening of *South Pacific* on April 7, 1949, there was a feeling that it would be a hit. While there were many things that could have turned *Oklahoma!* into a failure, Rodgers and Hammerstein were always convinced that *South Pacific* was failure-proof. It was, as Hammerstein honestly admitted, "a potpourri of good theatrical elements."

The show opens on a colorful South Sea island setting with two native children singing a song in French. Suddenly the audience is aware of a major complication when the two principal characters, Nellie and Emile, enter and reveal their love. But these are not conventional lovers. The man is a middle-aged, worldly Frenchman, and the girl is a happy-go-lucky American. "These two people," Hammerstein once said, "have nothing in common but their love."

Nellie responds to her feelings in typical, direct fashion. She is, she admits, "A Cockeyed Optimist" who is "stuck (like a dope!) with a thing called hope." Her mood, mirrored in Rodgers' bright and skipping music, tells both de Becque *and* the audience exactly what they want to know about the girl. In addition, the song develops naturally from the dialogue and fits the character perfectly. De Becque, too, reveals what kind of a man he is in his first song. But as a cultured gentleman, he expresses himself in a more operatic manner through the aria "Some Enchanted Evening." We know now that he is deeply romantic and impulsive, and that his feeling for the girl is sincere. Right away, the situation captures the proper note of contrast to create an immediate audience sympathy toward the two lovers.

Thus, with no time lost, the mood is established. Presently, the play makes us aware of an even deeper contrast than age and background. When he was very young, de Becque had killed a man in France, and had run away to the islands. He prospered as a planter and fell in love with a Polynesian woman. When Emile tells Nellie this, and also that the two native children living with him are really his own children, she is shocked and runs away. At the end of *South Pacific*, she comes to realize that her love for Emile is stronger than her prejudice. "What we're saying," Hammerstein has explained, "is that all this prejudice that we have is something that fades away in the face of something that's really important."

In the second love story in *South Pacific*, Lieutenant Cable, a young officer from a respectable family, falls in love with a beautiful Polynesian girl who cannot even speak English. When Nellie asks him to explain to de Becque that prejudices are born in people, the lieutenant answers her in the song "Carefully Taught." In it, he explains that people's hatred toward other people is not born but must be learned. The song was a daring one to be part of a musical, but, despite warnings, Rodgers and Hammerstein insisted that it remain in the score. It expressed, of course, a feeling that both men shared. Their hopeful outlook on life stemmed directly from their belief in the basic goodness of man. They were not blind to people's feelings, but they felt strongly that the evil that men do and think is largely the result of attitudes and prejudices that they are taught as children. Hammerstein always said that his optimism was due to his being aware of people's faults—including his own. The person who starts out thinking that everyone is wonderful, he felt, soon receives many shocks that turn him into the deepest kind of cynic.

Not all of *South Pacific* is concerned with serious themes. No more rollicking song has been written for the theatre than "There Is Nothin' Like a Dame" which the sailors and Seabees sing. And there is Nellie's straightforward confession, "I'm In Love with a Wonderful Guy." This is the perfect way for a simple girl like Nellie to think of the man she's in love with—even if he is a sophisticated Frenchman.

Such a lighthearted, lilting song also let Hammerstein indulge in a bit more rhyming that usual. Notice the way he used a number of rapid rhymes—including interior rhymes—to help built up the excitement of the girl's emotion: "gay"–"dai(sy)"–"May"–"cliché"; and then "bright"–"night"–"light." In this way the listener is all set for the thrilling, arm-flinging finale as the girl gaily repeats the "I'm in love" phrase five times. Note, too, the first line in the song, "I'm as corny as Kansas in August." Hammerstein was inspired to write it while thinking of Mary Martin wearing a gingham dress in a scene from a show she had done a few years before. That was the musical, *One Touch of Venus,* in which she had played the goddess Venus during most of the evening, but then, at the end, came out as a mortal. Her naïveté and corn-fed quality in that scene made Hammerstein want to write a part for her that would fit that personality. Nellie Forbush turned out to be that part, and "I'm as corny as Kansas in August" was her perfect self-description. Hammerstein admitted that he had first thought of saying "corny as Arkansas" which was where Nellie came from, but he liked the comic sound of the two sharp "k's" in "corny" and "Kansas." And, after all, Kansas is the state most associated with corn.

"Younger Than Springtime" shows Rodgers and Hammerstein at the height of their power in creating an emotional song about young love. It is sung by Cable to the native girl, Liat, and in it he pours out his heart in a rich, expressive melody. Hammerstein's lyric again combines love with nature and with music. To Cable, holding the girl in his arms is like holding the world, and he describes her as being warmer than the winds of June and sweeter than music.

"Younger Than Springtime" is a rare example of a song being used in a Rodgers and Hammerstein show that had not been purposely written for that show. One day, about five or six years before writing the music for *South Pacific,* Rodgers was trying out a new melody at his piano. He soon forgot about it, but his daughter Mary liked the tune and remembered it. While working on *South Pacific,* he received a telephone call from Hammerstein. They had previously been discussing the kind of song Cable should sing to Liat, and Hammerstein was calling to tell him that not only were the words ready but the music was ready as well. "Have you suddenly become a composer, too?" Rodgers asked. "No," his partner replied. "I heard Mary whistling an old tune of yours, and I've added the words to it. I think it's just what we need for Joe Cable."

"Bali Ha'i" is an exceptionally important song in *South Pacific* since it supplies a theme for the islands and reveals their hypnotic power. Specifically, it is about the island called Bali Ha'i, the one special island for everyone's special hopes and special dreams. The haunting sound of the first three notes is almost all that is needed to establish the spellbinding appeal of the South Seas paradise, and the words perfectly match its mystical quality.

Rodgers' speed in composing is famous, but no song was ever written more swiftly than "Bali Ha'i." One evening while the composer was having dinner with a few friends at Joshua Logan's apartment, the lyricist rushed in with his finished lyric. Rodgers merely moved the dishes to one side, and quickly went over the typewritten words that his partner had handed him. He then turned the piece of paper over, took a pencil from his pocket, and began to put down the notes for the song. It took no more than five minutes for him to have the entire song completed.

The major contribution of *South Pacific* was its authors' ability to deal with important issues within the framework of the commercial musical theatre. This was not a musical with a message. This was a musical with a point of view. Its main purpose was to entertain audiences by telling a good story, but this did not mean that it should not make people think. The theme of brotherhood, of the need for people to understand one another, was an important part of the plot. Because Rodgers and Hammerstein and Logan were careful to keep it that way, no one could accuse them of pleading for a special cause. Their only cause was good theatre, and everything that went into *South Pacific* helped to make it good theatre.

CHAPTER 12

The King and I

"THE TROUBLE IS that people aren't interested in whether it's a good show or a bad show; they want to know whether it's better than *South Pacific.*" That was Richard Rodgers being quoted in 1950 about a musical play he and Oscar Hammerstein were working on at the time. It was called *The King and I.*

Success, of course, does have this built-in problem. People are bound to compare any subsequent work with a current hit. But Rodgers and Hammerstein obviously could not stop writing just because they had been successful before. The only thing for them to do was exactly what they did do. They continued to write musical plays about subjects that interested them. Though they hoped audiences would agree with their taste, they could only be true to themselves. As Rodgers once said, "I think it is disaster to try to do what the public wants, if you don't feel that way yourself." To which Hammerstein added, "You can't deliberately say, 'I will please the public although I don't like what I'm doing.' I think that's impossible. There must be a faith behind every work."

The King and I gave the partners the opportunity to continue writing about a theme that concerned them deeply—the necessity for people of one group to get along with people of another. The new play dealt with prejudice and suspicion on the part of both the East and the West. What the musical tries to say is that all race and color fade when there is mutual respect and understanding. Furthermore, *The King and I* had important things to say about tyranny and freedom. It showed how a ruler gradually changed from believing himself to be an all-powerful monarch to understanding the importance of making his country more democratic.

This changing attitude of an Oriental king comes as a result of the influence of an English schoolteacher, Anna Leonowens. The original Anna was a real person who had lived during the mid-1800s, and it was from her diaries that Margaret Langdon in 1944 had written the book *Anna and the King of Siam.* In spite of her influence, however, there is no romance between Anna and the king in the musical. It is obvious that they grow to have great respect and affection for each other, but it is never shown directly on the stage. "In dealing with them musically," Rodgers and Hammerstein once wrote, "we could not write songs that said 'I love you' or even 'I love her' or 'I love him.' We were dealing with two characters who could indulge themselves only in oblique expressions of their feelings. This is because they themselves did not realize what those feelings were."

Thus, *The King and I* turned out to be a truly meaningful musical play. It dealt with serious themes and complex characters. And it did it without being patronizing. Although the play had humor, it was far from being the unreal, extravagant type of Oriental musical of the past. Said Rodgers at the time: "Neither Oscar nor I wanted enamel-faced little things running out on stage with forefingers thrust upward giving out with 'ching-aling-aling.' "

A particularly challenging aspect of *The King and I* was the music. This was the first play that Rodgers and Hammerstein had written in which none of the characters was an American. Most of them were Siamese, which meant that Rodgers' job was to compose a good deal of music with an Oriental flavor. Yet the melodies had to be attractive to Western ears because the play was being presented before Western audiences. Rodgers was convinced that an evening of tinkling bells and gongs—even if he could write that kind of music—would drive the people into the street long before the final curtain went down.

The composer has compared his approach to the music to the way the American artist Grant Wood might paint a series of scenes in Bangkok, the capital of Siam. His paintings of the people and the buildings would certainly be accurate, but they would also look as if they had been seen through the eyes of a man whose roots went deep into American soil.

Rodgers' ability to blend his Orientally colored music with songs sung by the non-Siamese resulted in a beautifully balanced score. And Hammerstein's lyrics were notable for their poetic vision and dramatic power. The principal piece created with an Asian flavor is the charming orchestral number, "The March of the Siamese Children." It is used to accompany the large number of the king's children as they are being presented to their new English schoolteacher. At the entrance of Chulalongkorn, the crown prince, the music becomes louder and bolder, but then becomes softer for the last and smallest child in the group. The ballet "The Small House of Uncle Thomas" artfully combines the Far Eastern setting with the story of *Uncle Tom's Cabin* to point up the conflict between tyranny and freedom.

Like Billy Bigelow in *Carousel*, the king also has a soliloquy,

"A Puzzlement." This is a very different kind of song from the emotional outpouring of the barker in the previous play. To express the character of the complex monarch, Rodgers created a light, staccato rhythm that is perfectly suited to the king's clipped Oriental accent. Apart from having amusing lines, the song exposes all the doubts that the ruler already had about his power. Such problems as whether or not to form alliances with neighboring countries or what to tell his oldest son about women are understandable and human. They help to create a truly well-rounded character.

Among the songs not written with an Oriental flavor, the delicate waltz "Hello, Young Lovers," which Anna sings, is a beautiful combination of words and music. After being told about an unhappy young couple who are forbidden to fall in love, Anna is reminded of her own love for her late husband, Tom. Thinking of Tom makes her recall the pleasures of her youth—the earth smelling of summer, the sky being streaked with white, and the mist on an English hillside. Strengthened by her own years of happiness, Anna counsels the new lovers to be firm in their love and not to feel sorry for her. She is happy because her memories are happy.

Even in a lighter mood, Rodgers and Hammerstein were able to say important things. To the bubbly rhythm of "I Whistle a Happy Tune," they offered the advice that a person can really become brave by making believe he is brave. The song is a variation on the theme of "You'll Never Walk Alone"—only done with humor and sparkle.

As in any well-integrated score, the songs of *The King and I* have important things to say about the play's theme of brotherhood, and they are skillfully used to advance the story. The idea that people of different nationalities can get to like each other by knowing each other is effectively presented by Anna to her royal pupils in "Getting to Know You." This, however, is only implied. The song fits the situation and serves the purpose of the story. It was never intended as a "message" song, but it does offer an affirmative answer to Cable's "Carefully Taught" in *South Pacific*.

One of the most effectively staged scenes in all of the Rodgers and Hammerstein plays occurs after Anna and the king have had a fight about whether Anna is to have her own home or continue to live in the palace. Alone in her room, she releases all of her emotions in "Shall I Tell You What I Think of You?" in which she addresses her angry remarks to the absent monarch. As soon as the song is ended, Lady Thiang, the king's number one wife, enters and pleads with Anna to remain. Nothing she says can make the slightest impression on the schoolteacher, who is determined to take the next ship back to England. Then, as a final effort, Thiang sings "Something Wonderful." The song, while admitting all the king's faults, tells of his dreams and plans for his people. Thiang also expresses her own belief that with Anna's help he will be able to achieve "something wonderful." The combination of music and lyrics accomplishes what words alone could not do. Anna decides to remain.

In spite of the difficulties of locale and characters that Rodgers and Hammerstein faced in *The King and I*, most people in the theatre felt optimistic about the play's chances. For apart from the now impressive Rodgers and Hammerstein record, the musical was to star the radiant English actress, Gertrude Lawrence. In a way, it was she who was most responsible for the partners writing the play.

Ever since they had read the book *Anna and the King of Siam*, Rodgers' wife Dorothy and Hammerstein's wife Dorothy tried to get their husbands to adapt the story into a musical. But they met with no success. Later when they saw Irene Dunne and Rex Harrison in the motion picture version, Rodgers and Hammerstein began to think more seriously about it. However, the person who really started things moving was a literary agent, Helen Strauss, of the William Morris Agency. Miss Strauss, who was Miss Landon's agent, first brought the idea to Gertrude Lawrence. When the actress showed interest in the role, Miss Strauss arranged to have Miss Landon's publisher confer with Rodgers and Hammerstein. Contracts were signed even before the authors had settled on a title.

Though this was February, 1950, it was not until the following January that an actor was signed to play the king. Among those who were considered for the part were Rex Harrison (there were some doubts about his singing ability), José Ferrer, Ezio Pinza, Macdonald Carey, and Alfred Drake (he turned down the part). One day, Rodgers and Hammerstein attended an audition in which many singers and actors were trying out for the important role. The one who most interested them was a bald-headed young man who sat cross-legged on the stage and sang a strange Russian Gypsy song accompanying himself on the guitar. That was the first time the authors had seen or heard of Yul Brynner. "That's our king!" they both exclaimed, and Brynner was signed almost on the spot.

The King and I opened on March 29, 1951. It became the third Rodgers and Hammerstein play to run more than 1,000 performances on Broadway. During the run, Miss Lawrence died of cancer, and was succeeded as Anna by Constance Carpenter, and later by Patricia Morison.

In *The King and I*, Rodgers and Hammerstein again proved that by being true to themselves they were also being true to the theatregoing public. Their success with a play so different from anything else they had done before gave special meaning to one of their most cherished beliefs. Just before the opening of *The King and I*, they wrote: "Writers who repeat themselves will eventually bore themselves. And this condition is a short and automatic step toward boring the public."

CHAPTER 13

Victory at Sea and Me and Juliet

No NEW Rodgers and Hammerstein musicals opened in 1952. Yet, as far as Richard Rodgers was concerned, the year was an especially satisfying one. In January, the eleven-year-old *Pal Joey* by Rodgers and Hart was revived and turned into one of the biggest hits of the season. In October, the first episode of *Victory at Sea* was shown on television.

Victory at Sea was a dream of television producer Henry Salomon. He planned a documentary to be composed of film clips of all the major naval engagements during World War II. Sixty million feet of film were eventually used from ten different countries, Axis as well as Allies.

The program was divided into 26 half-hour segments. Therefore, when Rodgers agreed to compose the background score, he was committing himself to write a piece of music lasting 13 hours. This would make it almost equal in length to the entire *Ring* cycle of operas by Richard Wagner.

What Rodgers achieved was an impressive collection of

atmospheric themes that greatly enhanced the dramatic value of the individual episodes. "The Guadalcanal March" has since been frequently performed by marching bands, and other themes have become equally popular through the success of the recordings of the score.

One of the themes, "Beneath the Southern Cross," even turned up the following year as a song in a Rodgers and Hammerstein musical. Its new title was "No Other Love" and its engaging melody and expressive words became the hit song of *Me and Juliet*. The show opened in New York in May, 1953.

Rodgers had been thinking of doing a musical like *Me and Juliet* for a long while. Because both he and Hammerstein had been stagestruck from childhood, they resented the unreal image of the theatre held by so many people. What the partners wanted to do was to create a completely truthful backstage musical. They had both written plays about the theatre before—Rodgers with *Babes In Arms* and Hammerstein with *Music In the Air* and *Very Warm For May*—and this would give them another chance to write about a subject that they knew so intimately.

Hammerstein was also glad to be able to write his first original script since *Allegro*. But this time he would not be concerned very much with serious matters. The show would be light and amusing, and something entirely different from the previous Rodgers and Hammerstein musicals. To emphasize this, *Me and Juliet* was purposely called "A Musical Comedy" on the program, not "A Musical Play," which was the customary designation of the partners' works.

Most of the authentic touches in *Me and Juliet* stemmed from Rodgers and Hammerstein's personal experiences. The show was, as they explained, their "Valentine to Show Business," and it contained many of the pleasures and the problems that they recalled in the theatre. For their hero, they had an assistant stage manager working on his first show—just the kind of job Hammerstein had had when he first went into the professional theatre in 1917.

You're In Love, the show that he had worked on then, even provided him with an incident that he used in *Me and Juliet*. He had never forgotten the night he was standing backstage talking to one of the chorus girls. Suddenly, a chorus boy rushed up to them and asked the girl to give him some of her mascara. Young Hammerstein was taken aback by this odd request until he realized what the boy wanted the mascara for. He rubbed some off the girl's eyelash with his finger, bent down, and used it to cover up a hole in his black silk socks. Hammerstein always remembered this demonstration of fast thinking. When the right moment came in *Me and Juliet*, he put it in the show.

Using incidents from real life gave *Me and Juliet* an honesty few other backstage stories have ever had. The show was careful to avoid any situation that had already become well known through overexposure in so many movie musicals. "We were religious in keeping away from the trite things," Hammerstein said at the time. "You know, the kindly old stage doorman that everyone called 'Pop,' and the pretty little understudy who replaced the star on opening night. We also steered clear of telling the usual story about a company putting on a new show, with all the anxieties of the actors and producers."

"There are so many clichés about the theatre," Rodgers added. "Like most theatre people are jealous, temperamental goons. That a chorus girl is stupid. She isn't. A girl who comes to audition for us is an expert, an accomplished dancer or singer. She is someone who studied hard. Through her training she can beat out anyone applying without a real background."

What also intrigued Rodgers and Hammerstein was the chance to do a musical that would take place within one basic location. Here it would be a theatre where a show, *Me and Juliet*, is currently running on Broadway. In this way, the authors could go from place to place within the theatre to tell their story—backstage, onstage, in the lounge, in the dressing rooms, in the theatre manager's office, in the alleyway outside the stage door, in the orchestra pit, even on the electrician's bridge above the stage where the lighting is controlled.

One sequence is especially inventive. In the first act, the chief electrician hears the orchestra below begin to play "Keep It Gay," and he starts to sing it on the light bridge hanging about twelve feet above the stage. As soon as he finishes, the lights go out. They go on again beneath the bridge, and the audience sees the same number performed by the dancers during an actual performance of the "play-within-a-play." This sequence is then interrupted when the lights go out again. Within seconds the dancers are shown again, but this time in practice clothing continuing the same dance on a bare stage during a rehearsal. Thus, three scenes were shown during the course of only one musical number.

Hammerstein considered a number like this to be a good example of the importance of the librettist in the theatre. He gladly gave chief credit for the effect to the scenery designer, Jo Mielziner, and to choreographer Robert Alton. But he also took some of the credit for it. He had been the one to ask for the effect because it was important in the telling of his story.

There is a general lighthearted quality about the songs for *Me and Juliet*. The innocent optimism of youth—as revealed in "A Very Special Day"—sets the tone right from the start. "Keep It Gay" is advice that both writers made sure to follow.

Three songs deal directly with the theatre and the people in it. "It's Me" is a tripping little number that shows how appearing on the stage miraculously changes a tired, dull girl into a "delectable dame cool as cream and hotter than flame." A more serious view of the theatre is contained in a dramatic piece about the most important thing in an actor's life—the audience. The song calls the audience "The Big Black Giant," and Rodgers' music is purposely strong and heavy the way a giant should be. Though this giant may look the same at every performance, he is constantly changing. He may be laughing or weeping or coughing or sleeping, but he must be pleased. Because without him there is no theatre.

In a more satirical vein, Rodgers and Hammerstein had fun with their big black giant in "Intermission Talk." All of the silly chatter that goes on in the smoking lounge is caught in overheard bits of conversation. This then leads into the eternal theme of "The theatre is dying," sung by a group of "happy mourners." The authors, however, will have none of their pessimism. There will always be plays to see and actors to applaud, they maintain. And through the voices of other theatregoers, they drown out the mourners by insisting, "The theatre is living!"

Rodgers and Hammerstein were always optimistic about the future of the theatre. But Hammerstein was careful to point out exactly what kind of theatre he felt would last. "There was a time when the theatre did die," he once wrote, "and it remained dead for several centuries. The Romans killed it by bringing extreme realism into the theatre to such an extent that they actually shed blood on the stage. People stopped going. The theatre really did not come back until it was revived in churches through the miracle plays. There is a lesson in this. The greatest eras in the theatre have reflected something beyond literal imitation of life. They have been dominated by nobility of spirit, as in the Greek period, or the beauty of the word, as in the Elizabethan period. The theatre, at its best, is a nightly miracle."

Me and Juliet, in spite of its freshness and its authentic theatrical atmosphere, did not succeed as well as most Rodgers and Hammerstein musicals. Its run was only a little longer than the run of *Allegro*. Perhaps the main problem was in combining the real story with the story of the play-within-a-play. Also, the story at times was too melodramatic to be completely believable.

Nevertheless, the work contained many thoughts about the theatre that were well worth expressing. Furthermore, the authors proved that they could write a modern musical comedy with the style and imagination that was part of everything they did in the theatre.

CHAPTER 14

Pipe Dream and Cinderella

Perhaps *Pipe Dream* was one musical that Rodgers and Hammerstein never should have written. It was just not their kind of play. What attracted them to it was the challenge of doing the unexpected, but *Pipe Dream* was not only a change of pace, it was a change of direction.

The musical was based on the novel *Sweet Thursday* by John Steinbeck. Its characters were the lazy and shiftless people who lived in Cannery Row, in Monterey, California. Steinbeck had lived among these people and knew them well. But they were strangers to Rodgers and Hammerstein, no matter how much they admired Steinbeck's book. "Most of them are a little crazy," they once wrote. "But one of the reasons they stimulate us is because we haven't met them before in our work. Their problems are simple ones like the next meal, or how to get their best friend married to a somewhat unlikely girl."

Of course, the authors could only treat the characters in

their own individual way. The fault of *Pipe Dream* probably was that Rodgers and Hammerstein were too gentlemanly to deal with the strange variety of misfits, drunkards, and brawlers that made up the novel.

Making *Sweet Thursday* into a musical was first thought of by the producing team of Cy Feuer and Ernest Martin. When they were unable to get Frank Loesser to write the score, they suggested the idea to Rodgers and Hammerstein. The partners agreed to do it, and Feuer and Martin turned over all their rights.

As in every one of their plays, there is a good deal of the philosophy of Rodgers and Hammerstein in *Pipe Dream.* Though the characters are lowlifes, they are treated with much affection and understanding. The very first song in the musical, "All Kinds of People," revealed a favorite Rodgers and Hammerstein theme. Whether we like it or not, the song tells us, it takes all kinds of people to make up a world. Everyone can learn something by studying even the lowest forms of animal life.

Rodgers and Hammerstein have frequently been accused of loving people too much. This just isn't true. As Rodgers has said, "We don't say everybody has to love each other. We just say that they might give a thought to trying to understand each other. Because no matter how people think or feel, there will still be all kinds of people on this earth."

Although they hardly were in agreement with the day-to-day philosophy of the play's characters, the team wrote a clever, rollicking piece, "A Lopsided Bus," to express the attitude of the happy-go-lucky bums. Somehow or other, these drifters manage to get by to meet the next day, and the music mirrors the bumpy road that they have to travel. Also, being simple people, they reveal their happiness in simple pleasures. All it takes is the sun flying in the window or the wind whispering through a tree to bring on a happy, careless "Sweet Thursday."

The main character of *Pipe Dream* is Doc, a scientist who runs a commercial biological laboratory. He befriends an innocent young waif named Suzy and, urged on by his buddies, eventually falls in love and marries her. Suzy's first song, "Everybody's Got a Home But Me," shows her to be a girl with a hidden desire for security. She likes her free and easy life, but now and then she dreams of how nice it would be to have her own home somewhere, and to enjoy the contentment of belonging to someone. This theme recurs frequently in Hammerstein's lyrics. It is a very fundamental emotion, just the kind that he always believed a song should express. "People are interested in yearning for home," he once wrote. "It's a mythical little white house on a green lawn, full of peace and freedom from care."

The main ballad in *Pipe Dream* is Doc's song, "All at Once," which he sings to Suzy. An intimate, tender expression, it is somewhat similar to the love-at-first-sight theme that was more ardently expressed in "Some Enchanted Evening." The couple's final duet, "The Next Time It Happens," reveals their deep love by having them vow that they will be more careful the next time they fall in love. They both realize, however, that it would take a miracle for them to feel this way again.

Though given a careful production, *Pipe Dream* lasted only 246 performances on Broadway to make it the shortest-running Rodgers and Hammerstein musical. Audiences were very much aware that there were too many miles separating the world of Cannery Row from the world of Rodgers and Hammerstein.

There were other things on Richard Rodgers' mind to make the relative failure of *Pipe Dream* seem unimportant. In the spring of 1955, Rodgers had complained of what he thought was a toothache. After an examination, it was discovered to be cancer of the jaw. He was successfully operated on in September, 1955, just two months before *Pipe Dream* opened. However, he was in constant pain throughout rehearsals and the tryout performances.

Rodgers felt that his recovery was greatly helped by his own mental attitude. He simply told the doctors, "I'm going to lick this." Only ten days after the operation, he went to a rehearsal of *Pipe Dream*, though he was still staying at the hospital. Working on the show helped take his mind off his illness. "Surrounded by health and youth and their passion to succeed," he wrote, "my own determination had to match theirs."

But the greatest satisfaction to Richard Rodgers was his ability to do a new score. The doctors had pronounced him completely cured, but he had no idea how his illness had affected his power to create music. The test came with *Cinderella*, which he and Oscar Hammerstein wrote especially for television. It was presented on one evening only, March 31, 1957, exactly fourteen years after the New York opening of *Oklahoma!*

Julie Andrews' agent was the first to think of Rodgers and Hammerstein adapting the fairy tale as a musical for his client. Miss Andrews, who was then starring in the most successful version of the Cinderella legend, *My Fair Lady*, had already played the part in an English pantomime production. Rodgers and Hammerstein liked the idea, and it wasn't long before the Columbia Broadcasting System happily announced that it would be presented coast-to-coast as a 90-minute "special."

From the start, the authors decided that the only way to do a new *Cinderella* was to stick as closely as possible to the old *Cinderella*. When asked where he had read the tale, Hammerstein replied honestly, "I looked it up in an encyclopedia. We want the kids to recognize the story they know. Children can be very critical about that. But since their parents will be watching too, we have tried to make the characters more human."

In order to do this, Hammerstein purposely made the fairy godmother a rather down-to-earth young lady. She is pretty and she has a sense of humor. In her first scene with Cinderella, she even tries to talk the starry-eyed slavy out of her wild desire to go to the ball. However, it is Cinderella's innocent faith in a miracle—expressed in the song "Impossible"—that finally persuades the godmother to give in and grant the wish. Another slight change was in making the stepsisters more laughable than cruel.

The score for *Cinderella* represents Rodgers and Hammerstein in a lighthearted and charming mood. Cinderella's first song, "In My Own Little Corner," lets her use her imagination to dream of all the exciting things she would like to do if she ever got the chance. When the Prince finally meets Cinderella, he serenades her with two ardent love songs, "Ten Minutes Ago" and "Do I Love You Because You're Beautiful?" The first has the lilt and glow of a true fairy-tale ballad. The second is full of youthful ardor as he asks the lover's eternal question: Does he love Cinderella because she is beautiful, or is she beautiful because he loves her? The score also has three purely orchestral pieces, a march for the stepsisters, a "Gavotte" and a "Waltz for the Ball," that are as lovely as anything Rodgers has ever written.

Rodgers and Hammerstein tried to approach their work for *Cinderella* in the same way that they would a regular stage production. The seven months they worked on the show were about equal to the nine months to a year that they usually spent in preparing a musical for Broadway. The rehearsals at the actual studio were like out-of-town tryouts. They also had commercial recordings made of the songs so that they could get some idea of the reactions before the telecast took place.

When *Cinderella* was shown across the country, surveys showed that it was seen by as many as 75 to 100 million people. This means that more than twice as many people saw Rodgers and Hammerstein's single television musical than had viewed all of their previous Broadway productions.

CHAPTER 15

Flower Drum Song

Rodgers and Hammerstein were very close to the members of the Fields family—both socially and professionally. The family consisted of Lew Fields and his children, Herbert, Dorothy, and Joseph. Lew Fields had given Rodgers his first opportunity in the theatre, and had produced many of his early hits. Herbert had been the librettist for eight Rodgers and Hart shows. Together, Dorothy and Herbert had written the book for *Annie Get Your Gun* which was produced by Rodgers and Hammerstein. Joseph started his musical comedy career in 1949 when he was co-author of *Gentlemen Prefer Blondes.*

While living in Hollywood where he produced and wrote for the screen, Joe Fields read and admired a novel called *The Flower Drum Song* by Chin Y. Lee. Early in 1958, he secured the rights to turn the novel into a play. Luckily, Oscar Hammerstein was on the West Coast at the time. At Fields' suggestion, Hammerstein read the book, liked it, and immediately began to see the musical comedy possibilities. Once Rodgers gave his approval, the three men formed a partnership to produce the work on the stage, with Fields joining Hammerstein as co-author.

The story that they adapted takes place in San Francisco's Chinatown, and is concerned with the conflict between the older and the younger generations of Chinese. The title refers to the traditional song of the Chinese strolling minstrels which is accompanied by the beating of a traditional flower drum. "There isn't much plot to the novel," Hammerstein admitted shortly before the musical's opening, "but it's strong on character and background, like a Chinese *Life With Father*. I just fell in love with it."

Flower Drum Song, like *South Pacific* and *The King and I*, gave Rodgers and Hammerstein the chance to write again about Oriental people. It also allowed them to deal with a recurring theme: People should learn to get along with other people. Here, however, this theme applied only to the need for the older, more traditional Chinese to get along with the younger, more Americanized Chinese, and vice versa. The approach dealt mostly with the humorous aspects of this adjustment, with perhaps a bit too much of the stock concept of Orientals allowed to creep in.

In adapting the book, Hammerstein and Fields put the domineering father, Wang Ch-Yang, slightly in the background to bring out the love stories involving the younger people. The two leading female parts were Mei Li, a mail-order bride from China, and Linda Low, a Chinese-American honky-tonk dancer. Both these parts were played by actresses of Japanese ancestry, Miyoshi Umeki and Pat Suzuki. The story is concerned with the way Mei Li, who is supposed to marry Sammy Fong, is able to get Wang Ta to marry her. Wang, however, thinks he loves Linda. Eventually all the complications are smoothed out and Mei Li marries Wang Ta, and Linda marries Sammy.

Using two contrasting love stories with opposite-type girls is a theatrical device that gives a play balance. It helps to move the action from romantic to comic situations, which is necessary in the musical theatre. *Oklahoma!* had the sweet Laurie Williams and the boy-crazy Ado Annie Carnes. In *Carousel*, the outwardly calm Julie Jordan balanced the emotional Carrie Pipperidge. *South Pacific* contrasted "Knuckle-head" Nellie Forbush with the shy native girl, Liat. The inexperienced understudy, Jeanie, was matched by the aggressive dancer, Betty, in *Me and Juliet*. This technique had a special appeal in *Flower Drum Song* chiefly because both girls were Oriental.

The music in the play also allowed for a contrast between the more traditional Chinese type and the more native American type. "You Are Beautiful," which was supposed to be based on an ancient Chinese poem, has a gliding, delicate melody to suggest the movement of a flower boat. Its sentiment is basically love at first sight, but it achieves a rare poetic quality through its music and its simple imagery. In it, for example, a girl's laugh is compared to the fall of lotus leaves brushing the air of night.

From another supposedly traditional source, "A Hundred Million Miracles" is performed as a real flower drum song. These miracles do not make people rich or powerful. Hammerstein would have no use for that. His miracles are the simple ones that people too often overlook—a starlit sky, a bird flying out of an egg, a child's first attempt to walk, the sun coming up in the east. Hammerstein always felt that people needed to be reminded of such things. To him, it was a duty to oppose the belief of some writers that life is ugly and meaningless. He did not deny that that part of life exists. But he always tried to show that such things are not all there is to life, and that a hundred million unnoticed miracles do happen every day.

The fragile quality of "I Am Going to Like It Here," sung by Mei Li, gives this song a particularly Oriental quality. It uses a quiet, slightly singsong melody to express the feelings of a well-brought-up girl who realizes that she is beginning to fall in love. The lyric has a very unusual construction. Hammerstein wrote six stanzas for the song, five of which have four lines each, and the last one has six lines because the final two lines are repeated. The second and fourth line in each stanza becomes the first and third line in the following stanza in every case but the last. In other words, if we were to use a letter of the alphabet to stand for each line, the song would look like this:

A
B
C
D

B
E
D
F

E
G
F
H

G
I
H
J

I
K
J
L

K
M
N
O
N
O

Just as "A Hundred Millions Miracles" and "I Am Going to Like It Here" tell in their Oriental way about the sweet innocence of Mei Li, so "I Enjoy Being a Girl" tells all about the character of Linda Low. Linda's song is a lengthy soliloquy all about herself. She is "strictly a female female" who delights in all the things that appeal to a girl, such as a new hairdo, getting flowers, lace dresses, talking on the telephone for hours, and receiving compliments from men. Rodgers' music is properly brassy and direct, with suggestions of a waltz and a patriotic theme in perfect complement to the lyric.

Like most other musicals, *Flower Drum Song* had to undergo many changes during its tour before opening in New York. While in Boston, Rodgers and Hammerstein became convinced that the show needed a new song. They wanted a comic number for the character of Sammy Fong, a flashy young man, to sing to Mei Li, the girl he has agreed to marry. It took Hammerstein four days to come up with the words to the song which he called "Don't Marry Me." Rodgers received the words during a rehearsal at the Shubert Theatre. Since the regular piano was in use, he found another one in the ladies' room of the theatre. In spite of the activities going on at the rehearsal, he was able to create the music within a few hours. Almost immediately after Rodgers had finished the song, Larry Blyden, who was playing Sammy, was learning the music and lyrics. Just two nights later, he was singing "Don't Marry Me" in an actual performance.

The clever lyric and spirited music show how well Rodgers and Hammerstein could write in a purely musical comedy vein. The song is actually a reverse twist on the usual plea for marriage. Since Sammy wants Mei Li to free him from his agreement, he gaily lists all his bad qualities. As performed in bouncy style by Blyden and Miss Umeki, the applause-catching number quickly became an audience favorite.

The beauty of the production, which was staged by Gene Kelly, was a major attraction of *Flower Drum Song*. It opened on December 1, 1958, and ran for 600 performances. Though hardly in a class with *Oklahoma!*, *Carousel*, *South Pacific* or *The King and I*, it was a spirited and friendly show. Its skills may have been more in the telling than in the tale, but on its own musical comedy terms *Flower Drum Song* had a pleasantly endearing quality.

CHAPTER 16

The Sound of Music

Many things happen to a musical from the time someone gets the original idea to the time it opens in New York. Stories get changed, songs get added and songs get thrown out, actors may be replaced. Sometimes the show itself is forced to close on the road and never even has a New York opening. The only thing that is usually certain is that the people responsible for the show have faith in it.

The Sound of Music really needed the faith of everyone concerned. Even before the musical began to take shape, it ran into many serious roadblocks. In fact, by the time the show actually went into rehearsal it almost seemed as if those responsible for it really had to climb every mountain and ford every stream in order for *The Sound of Music* to be heard.

Rodgers and Hammerstein usually let about two years go by between musicals. Yet here they were in 1959, coming up with a new production just one year after *Flower Drum Song*.

[161

There was a special reason for this unaccustomed flurry of activity.

In the summer of 1955—more than four years before *The Sound of Music* opened—Mary Martin met a young director named Vincent J. Donehue. Soon afterward, he directed her in the television production of *The Skin Of Our Teeth*, and they became very close friends.

About a year later, Paramount Pictures asked Donehue to direct a new movie version of a German film that they had under option. The German film was called *The Trapp Family Singers*, and was based on the life of Baroness Maria von Trapp and her family. Its story told how, as a young girl, the baroness had prepared to become a nun in her native Austria. However, she gave up her religious life to become a governess for the seven children of Baron Georg von Trapp, a widower. Maria and the baron fell in love and were married. After Hitler's invasion of Austria, they escaped with their whole family to America, where they won new fame with their singing concerts.

As soon as he saw the German film, Donehue wanted to direct it—but not as a movie. He saw it only as a musical play with Mary Martin in the role of Maria. Once Paramount let its option drop, the director secured a print of the original movie, and had it shown to Miss Martin and her husband, Richard Halliday. They both saw the same possibilities in the story that Donehue did. Halliday agreed to produce the play for his wife, but first there was the matter of securing permission to dramatize the story on the stage.

This permission had to be won from the living members of the Trapp family and also from the German film company that had made the original movie based on their story. Halliday's first problem was to find the baroness, who was a widow, but she could not be located. The only information he could get was that she was somewhere in the South Pacific doing missionary work. After eight months of searching, the producer still could not find her.

One night, Halliday told Leland Hayward, who had co-produced *South Pacific*, all about his fruitless eight-month quest. Hayward became so fascinated by the project that he asked Halliday if he might join him in producing the musical. When Halliday agreed, Hayward promptly joined in the worldwide hunt to secure the theatrical rights.

Hayward's first task was to deal with the German film company about getting permission. It required six trips to Munich, where the company was located, before the movie executives were willing to come to terms. During one of these trips, Hayward was given information about Baroness von Trapp. She had been stricken with malaria in New Guinea, and had been flown to a hospital in Innsbrück, Austria. Hayward lost no time in visiting her. At first she was unwilling to allow her story to be turned into a Broadway musical, but when the producer explained that the money she would make from the show could be used to help her missions, the baroness accepted the offer. This still didn't give Halliday and Hayward all the necessary permissions. They now had to get approval from each one of the seven Trapp children to allow the producers to have them portrayed on the stage. The search for the children also took a long time, since they were living in many different countries.

Now with all the necessary permissions granted, the producers were at last able to turn their attention to finding writers for the musical. To create the libretto, they signed the experienced playwrighting team of Howard Lindsay and Russel Crouse. But what should they do about the songs? Originally, the idea was to use the actual folk songs that the Trapp family sang in concerts, plus a new song that Halliday and Hayward hoped Rodgers and Hammerstein would write.

When the producers told Rodgers about this idea, the composer objected to it. It would be impractical, he told them. "Either you do it authentically," he said, "and use all actual Trapp music, or you get a completely new score for it." It didn't take Halliday and Hayward long to make up their minds. Of course, they'd love to have Rodgers and Hammerstein write the entire score, and they would also welcome the partners as co-producers. But there was still one hitch: Rodgers and Hammerstein were then busily occupied with *Flower Drum Song*. Could the new show wait? "If you and Oscar will do the music and lyrics," the producers told Rodgers, "we will wait."

Luckily, the wait did not turn out to be long. On November 16, 1959—a little less than a year after the opening of *Flower Drum Song—The Sound of Music* opened in New York. At this writing, it is still running.

Although the Austrian locale of the musical was something new for the team of Rodgers and Hammerstein, it was, of course, familiar territory to Hammerstein. In particular, the countryside setting and the warmhearted characters were much in the spirit of *Music In the Air*, even though Hammerstein had nothing to do with the new story. Lindsay and Crouse, however, were well aware of the problems of writing a musical about people living in Austria. Too many people still think of it only as a setting for operetta. "We had to keep the story convincing and believable," Lindsay has said, "not letting it get into the never-never land that operetta lives in."

One of the things that helped make *The Sound of Music* convincing and believable was that the main conflict was based on fact—the opposition of many Austrians to the Nazis. However, this conflict never turns into a scene of actual fighting. The audience never even sees a Nazi. During the tryout tour, it was decided that the struggle would be far more effective if the Nazis, who were then in the show, were taken out. According to Rodgers, "The end result is that there's more menace without seeing them than there was when they were onstage in those musical comedy uniforms. Having them off-stage exerts more pressure on the situation than seeing them did."

Nevertheless, in spite of the reality of the situations in *The Sound of Music,* there were many who felt that the musical was coated too thickly with sentimentality. Hammerstein was quick to answer such charges. "Sentiment," he once said, "has never been unpopular except with a few sick persons who are made sicker by the sight of a child, a glimpse of a wedding, or the thought of a happy home. *The Sound of Music* is based on the autobiography of Maria von Trapp. The plot is no invention of ours. No incidents were invented or dragged in to play on the sentimental susceptibilities of the audience, as some critics seem to feel." To which Rodgers has added, "Most of us still feel that nature can have attractive manifestations, that children aren't necessarily monsters, and that deep affection between two people is nothing to be ashamed of. I feel that way rather strongly or obviously it would not be possible for me to write the music that goes with Oscar's words."

The words and music that the team wrote for *The Sound of Music* expressed many of the things that they felt most deeply about. The title song, which is the first one sung by Maria, has a beautifully romantic melody that captures all the open-air, openhearted charm of the words. Once again, as in "Oh, What a Beautiful Mornin'," the theme is the closeness of nature to music. The hills are alive with the sound of music, it tells us, and the beauty and variety of these sounds lift our hearts when we are lonely. "My Favorite Things" is a collection of all the simple delights of man and nature that go into making life more pleasant. The melody is appropriately bright and skipping as it accompanies the description of these delights. Then, in the middle part, or release, it abruptly becomes jarring to accompany such unfavorite things as the biting of a dog or the stinging of a bee. The gay children's march, "Do Re Mi," continues the favorite things idea by making certain things stand for the notes on a scale. And "An Ordinary Couple" paints the blissful picture of two people sharing the joys and problems of life. For them there is no greater happiness than watching the fading sun at the end of day with their arms around each other and their children by their side.

A great deal of the local Austrian color is found in the yodeling polka, "The Lonely Goatherd," and in the tender "Edelweiss," which was the last song written by Rodgers and Hammerstein. Since many scenes in *The Sound of Music* take place in Nonnberg Abbey, where Maria studied to be a nun, there are also pieces with a deeply religious feeling. The "Preludium," which is used instead of an overture, sets the proper mood for the opening scene in the abbey. Rodgers' music, sung by an a cappella choir, sounds so authentic that many people have taken it to be an ancient musical setting for the Catholic chant *Dixit Dominus*, rather than a new work.

The most dramatic in the religious vein is the hymnlike "Climb Every Mountain." Like Rodgers and Hammerstein's previous "You'll Never Walk Alone" from *Carousel*, the song is a moving expression of the power of faith—in this case, a faith strong enough to help a person climb mountains and ford streams. Note that Rodgers and Hammerstein did not say that the mountain will be climbed and the streams forded. They were well aware that life's problems are never simple. But they did say that sometimes great efforts are needed if our dreams are ever to come true.

This, of course, was a very deep conviction with Hammerstein. Everyone has to have a dream, or a faith, to carry him through the darkest times. And it was that kind of faith that helped to give Oscar Hammerstein the strength to carry on in his own life.

In September, 1959, just before rehearsals were to begin on *The Sound of Music*, Hammerstein began to feel abdominal pains. When it was discovered that he had an ulcer, he was operated on immediately. His recovery was fairly rapid, and he was able to join Rodgers in Boston during the musical's tryout tour.

Even though the pain did not go away, Hammerstein had the same determination to lick his illness that Rodgers had had when he was sick. "We went through the winter making believe everything was fine," Rodgers said. Hammerstein even felt well enough to go to London in March, 1960, for the opening of *Flower Drum Song*.

It was soon after this that Hammerstein began to fear the worst. In July, he went to a doctor and asked directly if he was going to die of cancer. When the doctor said yes, Hammerstein thought long and hard about the choices that he could take. He could possibly have prolonged his life by another operation or by X-ray treatments, but he knew that he would never be well again.

Therefore, he made a brave decision. He decided that he would calmly prepare for his death in the most peaceful surroundings he knew. He went back to his farm in the Pennsylvania hills. There he helped each member of his family to adjust to his death. He did not complain about his misfortune. He never showed fear.

Ever since his mother's death when he was fifteen years old, Oscar Hammerstein had fought against the grief that comes after death. When his own time came, he was just as determined to fight against any uncontrolled emotion. And by his own attitude, he gave his family the strength to continue without him.

Epilogue

On january 16, 1954, *South Pacific* gave its 1,925th and final Broadway performance. After the cast had taken its final bows, everyone joined in the singing of "Auld Lang Syne." Then, Myron McCormick, one of the featured actors, stepped to the footlights and announced that, as a symbol of its never-ending appeal, the final curtain would not be lowered on *South Pacific*. Likewise, the theatre of Rodgers and Hammerstein did not end with Hammerstein's death.

The legacy of the team was more than the sum of their stage successes. By daring to do things differently, they encouraged a whole new generation of writers to do things differently. Many of the most significant figures of the musical theatre readily admit the debt that they owe Rodgers and Hammerstein. It was not only that they dealt with serious subjects within the framework of light entertainment. It was their entire conception of the musical theatre as a place of ideas and even ideals. The fresh winds of *Oklahoma!* that had come sweeping down the plain had carried writers and audiences into an era of mature, intelligent musical theatre.

Rodgers and Hammerstein did more than give indirect encouragement. Their policy of holding frequent auditions and of awarding scholarships to music students showed their great concern with young people just getting started. To Rodgers, such encouragement is a form of continuity. "You want to continue," he has said. "First of all, you want to continue yourself in your children just by having them. You want to continue yourself in your work. The interest in other people's children and in other people's children's work is simply an extension of that drive."

Not only did Rodgers and Hammerstein help young people in the theatre, they even urged young people to go into the theatre. "Don't listen to those who say, 'Oh, don't go into the theatre, it's too hard,'" Hammerstein once wrote. "Anything good is too hard somewhere along the line. I do say that to be successful in the theatre, you must have an irrational love for it. It's not enough to have talent. Good theatre people are made up of a combination of ambition and industry as well as talent. I've seen some talented people who lack the staying power, the stamina, that the theatre requires."

In their own families, Rodgers and Hammerstein were understandably proud of their children's abilities in music and the theatre. Rodgers' daughter, Mary, wrote the score for the popular musical, *Once Upon a Mattress*, and his other daughter, Linda, also is a talented composer. Together, both girls once collaborated on a one-woman touring show for Mary Martin. Hammerstein's two sons, William and James, began their theatre careers as stage managers, as their father had done, and both have been active as producers and directors. James staged the Israeli production of *The King and I* in 1966, and William was responsible for directing the highly acclaimed Broadway production of *Oklahoma!* in 1979. Hammerstein's daughter, Alice, has written lyrics for television, films, and the theatre.

After Oscar Hammerstein's death, Rodgers himself continued the spirit of the theatre of Rodgers and Hammerstein.
In 1962, *No Strings* found the composer, who was writing his
own lyrics for the first time, showing an unmistakable link with
his late partner in such pieces as "The Sweetest Sounds," "Look
No Further," and "Maine." And while the production introduced daring innovations in stagecraft and in Samuel Taylor's
interracial love story, *No Strings* was concerned with the same
issues of personal integrity in the modern world that had been
the theme of *Allegro*.

Other shows found Rodgers working with various lyricists.
He joined with Stephen Sondheim, who had actually been
Hammerstein's protégé, for *Do I Hear a Waltz?*, a rueful
comedy set in present-day Italy. For *Two by Two*, which had
lyrics by Martin Charnin, he went back to the biblical tale of
Noah and his family, with Danny Kaye returning to Broad-
day as the ancient ark-builder. *Rex*, in 1976, brought Rodgers
together with Sheldon Harnick, but unfortunately their saga
of King Henry VIII was far less adaptable to the musical stage
than had been the saga of the King of Siam. Perhaps the closest
Rodgers came to recreating the world of Rodgers and Hammerstein was in his final work, *I Remember Mama*, which
opened in May 1979. Again collaborating with Martin Charnin, the composer created the music for a story that he had
once presented with Hammerstein as a play without music.
Starring Liv Ullmann, the sentimental tale of a Norwegian
family living in San Francisco at the turn of the century provided the atmosphere and theme for a score that was warm,
evocative, and highly personal.

Richard Rodgers died in New York on December 30, 1979,
after years of suffering the agonies of cancer of the jaw and
throat and a serious heart attack. As did the passing of Oscar
Hammerstein, his death at the age of 77 made people who had
known him only through his music feel as if they had lost a

close friend. In a tribute similar to that given his former partner, the lights of the Broadway theatre marquees were darkened for a minute in his honor.

Contrary to Shakespeare, the good that people do does live after them. Especially in the arts and especially in the art of Rodgers and Hammerstein. Their major contributions—*Oklahoma!*, *Carousel*, *South Pacific*, *The King and I*, *The Sound of Music*—are constantly being presented in regional theatres throughout the United States as well as in translations throughout the world. Film versions are regularly revived in movie theatres and on television. In 1977, a new production of *The King and I*, starring the original monarch, Yul Brynner, played to packed houses on Broadway; at this writing, with Brynner still in it, the musical continues to play to packed houses in London. Then, on December 13, 1979, just seventeen days before Rodgers' death, *Oklahoma!* came sweeping into New York in a spanking new production that once more had theatregoers queuing up at the boxoffice. After almost thirty-seven years, it was still the brightest, sunniest, most captivating musical of the season.

Lower the curtain on Rodgers and Hammerstein? Not a chance.

STANLEY GREEN
New York City
June 1980

APPENDIX

The following listing contains all the songs written by Rodgers and Hammerstein. Unless otherwise noted, Mr. Hammerstein is responsible for books and lyrics of all the musicals; Mr. Rodgers for the music. The singer who introduced each song is listed right after the title.

1920. "Room for One More"—William Towson Taylor
      From *Fly With Me*, Columbia University Varsity Show

1943. OKLAHOMA!
      Producer: The Theatre Guild
      Director: Rouben Mamoulian
      Choreographer: Agnes de Mille
      New York Run: March 31, 1943–May 29, 1948
      Performances: 2,212
      "Oh, What a Beautiful Mornin' "—Alfred Drake
      "The Surrey with the Fringe On Top"—Alfred Drake, Joan
          Roberts, Betty Garde
      "Kansas City"—Lee Dixon, Betty Garde
      "I Cain't Say No"—Celeste Holm
      "Many a New Day"—Joan Roberts

"It's a Scandal! It's a Outrage!"—Joseph Buloff
"People Will Say We're In Love"—Alfred Drake, Joan
   Roberts
"Pore Jud"—Alfred Drake, Howard daSilva
"Lonely Room"—Howard daSilva
"Out of My Dreams"—Joan Roberts
"The Farmer and the Cowman"—Ralph Riggs, Betty Garde,
   Alfred Drake, Lee Dixon, Celeste Holm, Edwin Clay,
   ensemble
"All er Nothin' "—Celeste Holm, Lee Dixon
"Oklahoma"—Alfred Drake, Joan Roberts, Betty Garde,
   Barry Kelley, Edwin Clay, ensemble
NOTE: "Boys and Girls Like You and Me" dropped before
   opening.

"The P.T.Boat Song" ("Steady as You Go")

1944. "Dear Friend" (for Fifth War Loan Drive)

"We're On Our Way" (Infantry Song)

1945. CAROUSEL
   Producer: The Theatre Guild
   Director: Rouben Mamoulian
   Choreographer: Agnes de Mille
   New York Run: April 19, 1945–May 24, 1947
   Performances: 890
   "Carousel Waltz"—Orchestra
   "You're a Queer One, Julie Jordan"—Jean Darling, Jan
      Clayton
   "Mister Snow—Jean Darling
   "If I Loved You"—John Raitt, Jan Clayton
   "June Is Bustin' Out All Over"—Christine Johnson, Jan
      Clayton, ensemble
   "When the Children Are Asleep"—Eric Mattson, Jean
      Darling

"Blow High, Blow Low"—Murvyn Vye, John Raitt, men
"Soliloquy"—John Raitt
"This Was a Real Nice Clambake"—Jean Darling, Christine
    Johnson, Jan Clayton, Eric Mattson, ensemble
"Geraniums In the Winder"—Eric Mattson
"There's Nothin' So Bad for a Woman"—Murvyn Vye
"What's the Use of Wond'rin' "—Jan Clayton
"You'll Never Walk Alone"—Christine Johnson
"The Highest Judge of All"—John Raitt

STATE FAIR
Studio: 20th Century-Fox
Producer: William Perlberg
Director: Walter Lang
Release Date: August 20, 1945
"Our State Fair"—Luanne Hogan (for Jeanne Crain), Dick
    Haymes, Charles Winninger, Fay Bainter
"It Might As Well Be Spring"—Luanne Hogan (for Jeanne
    Crain)
"That's for Me"—Vivian Blaine, Dick Haymes
"It's a Grand Night for Singing"—Vivian Blaine, ensemble
"Isn't It Kinda Fun?"—Dick Haymes
"All I Owe Ioway"—Ensemble
NOTE: "We Will Be Together" dropped before film was
    released.

1946. "I Haven't Got a Worry In the World"—Helen Hayes
    From *Happy Birthday*

1947. ALLEGRO
    Producer: The Theatre Guild
    Director-Choreographer: Agnes de Mille
    New York Run: October 10, 1947–July 10, 1948
    Performances: 315
    "Joseph Taylor, Jr."—Chorus
    "I Know It Can Happen Again"—Muriel O'Malley

"One Foot, Other Foot"—Annamary Dickey, Muriel
O'Malley, chorus
"Winters Go By"—Muriel O'Malley, chorus
"Poor Joe"—Chorus
"A Fellow Needs a Girl"—William Ching, Annamary
Dickey
"A Darn Nice Campus"—John Battles
"So Far"—Gloria Wills
"You Are Never Away"—John Battles
"What a Lovely Day for a Wedding"—Paul Parks, chorus
"It May Be a Good Idea"—John Conte
"To Have and to Hold"—Chorus
"Wish Them Well"—Chorus
"Money Isn't Everything"—Roberta Jonay, Kathryn Lee,
Patricia Bybell, Sylvia Karlton, Julie Humphries
"Yatata Yatata Yatata"—John Conte, chorus
"The Gentleman Is a Dope"—Lisa Kirk
"Allegro"—Lisa Kirk, John Battles, John Conte, chorus
"Come Home"—Annamary Dickey

1949. SOUTH PACIFIC
Producer: Rodgers and Hammerstein, Leland Hayward,
Joshua Logan
Libretto: Hammerstein and Joshua Logan
Director: Joshua Logan
New York Run: April 7, 1949–January 16, 1954
Performances: 1,925
"Dites-Moi"—Barbara Luna, Michael DeLeon
"A Cockeyed Optimist"—Mary Martin
"Twin Soliloquies"—Mary Martin, Ezio Pinza
"Some Enchanted Evening"—Ezio Pinza
"Bloody Mary"—Sailors, Seabees, Marines
"There Is Nothin' Like a Dame"—Henry Michel, Jim
Hawthorne, Thomas Gleason, Myron McCormick,
Dickinson Eastham, Biff McGuire, Henry Slate, Don
Fellows, Alan Gilbert

"Bali Ha'i"—Juanita Hall, Myron McCormick, William
     Tabbert
"I'm Gonna Wash That Man Right Outa My Hair"—
     Mary Martin, nurses
"A Wonderful Guy"—Mary Martin, nurses
"Younger Than Springtime"—William Tabbert
"Happy Talk"—Juanita Hall
"Honey Bun"—Mary Martin, Myron McCormick, ensemble
"Carefully Taught"—William Tabbert
"This Nearly Was Mine"—Ezio Pinza
NOTE: "Loneliness of Evening" and "My Girl Back Home"
     dropped before opening.

1951. THE KING AND I
Producer: Rodgers and Hammerstein
Director: John van Druten
Choreographer: Jerome Robbins
New York Run: March 29, 1951–March 20, 1954
Performances: 1,246
"I Whistle a Happy Tune"—Gertrude Lawrence, Sandy
     Kennedy
"My Lord and Master"—Doretta Morrow
"Hello, Young Lovers"—Gertrude Lawrence
"March of the Siamese Children"—Orchestra
"A Puzzlement"—Yul Brynner
"The Royal Bangkok Academy"—Gertrude Lawrence,
     king's wives, children
"Getting to Know You"—Gertrude Lawrence, king's wives,
     children
"We Kiss In a Shadow"—Doretta Morrow, Larry Douglas
"Shall I Tell You What I Think of You?"—Gertrude
     Lawrence
"Something Wonderful"—Dorothy Sarnoff
"Western People Funny"—Dorothy Sarnoff, king's wives
"I Have Dreamed"—Doretta Morrow, Larry Douglas
"The King's Song"—Yul Brynner

"Shall We Dance?"—Gertrude Lawrence, Yul Brynner
NOTE: "Waiting," "Who Would Refuse?" and "Now You Leave" dropped before opening.

1952. "Happy Christmas, Little Friend"

1953. ME AND JULIET
Producer: Rodgers and Hammerstein
Director: George Abbott
Choreographer: Robert Alton
New York Run: May 28, 1953–April 3, 1954
Performances: 358
"A Very Special Day"—Isabel Bigley
"That's the Way It Happens"—Isabel Bigley
"Marriage Type Love"—Arthur Maxwell, Helena Scott, ensemble
"Keep It Gay"—Mark Dawson
"The Big Black Giant"—Bill Hayes
"It's Me"—Joan McCracken, Isabel Bigley
"Intermission Talk"—Jackie Kelk, ensemble
"It Feels Good"—Mark Dawson
"The Baby You Love"—Helena Scott
"We Deserve Each Other"—Joan McCracken, Bob Fortier
"I'm Your Girl"—Isabel Bigley, Bill Hayes
NOTE: "The Baby You Love" dropped in June, 1953.

"There's Music In You"—Mary Martin
From *Main Street to Broadway* (film)

1955. PIPE DREAM
Producer: Rodgers and Hammerstein
Director: Harold Clurman
Choreographer: Boris Runanin
New York Run: November 30, 1955–June 30, 1956
Performances: 246
"All Kinds of People"—William Johnson, Mike Kellin

"The Tide Pool"–William Johnson, Mike Kellin, G. D. Wallace

"Everybody's Got a Home But Me"–Judy Tyler

"A Lopsided Bus"–G. D. Wallace, Mike Kellin, Jenny Workman, Annabelle Gold, Flophouse Gang

"Bums' Opera"–Helen Traubel, Kenneth Harvey, Ruby Braff, Flophouse Gang

"The Man I Used to Be"–William Johnson

"Sweet Thursday"–Helen Traubel

"Suzy Is a Good Thing"–Helen Traubel, Judy Tyler

"All at Once You Love Her"–William Johnson, Judy Tyler

"The Happiest House On the Block"–Helen Traubel, girls

"The Party That We're Gonna Have Tomorrow Night"– G. D. Wallace, ensemble

"The Party Gets Going"–Company

"I Am a Witch"–Helen Traubel, Temple Texas, Louise Troy, Mildred Slavin, Jackie McElroy

"Will You Marry Me?"–Judy Tyler, Helen Traubel, William Johnson

"Thinkin' "–Mike Kellin

"How Long?"–Helen Traubel, William Johnson, Flophouse Gang, girls

"The Next Time It Happens"–Judy Tyler, William Johnson

NOTE: "Sitting On the Back Porch" dropped before opening.

1957. CINDERELLA

Network: Columbia Broadcasting System

Producer: Richard Lewine

Director: Ralph Nelson

Choreographer: Jonathan Lucas

Single Performance: March 31, 1957

"Where Is Cinderella?"–Orchestra

"In My Own Little Corner"–Julie Andrews

"The Prince Is Giving a Ball"—Robert Penn, entire populace
"Impossible"—Julie Andrews, Edith Adams
"Gavotte"—Orchestra
"Ten Minutes Ago"—Julie Andrews, Jon Cypher
"Stepsisters' Lament"—Alice Ghostley, Kaye Ballard
"Waltz for a Ball"—Orchestra
"Do I Love You Because You're Beautiful?"—Jon Cypher and Julie Andrews
"A Lovely Night"—Julie Andrews, Ilka Chase, Alice Ghostley, Kaye Ballard
NOTE: "If I Weren't King" and "What's the Matter with the Man?" dropped before telecast.

1958. FLOWER DRUM SONG

Producer: Rodgers and Hammerstein, Joseph Fields
Libretto: Hammerstein and Joseph Fields
Director: Gene Kelly
Choreographer: Carol Haney
New York Run: December 1, 1958–May 7, 1960
Performances: 600
"You Are Beautiful"—Ed Kenney
"A Hundred Million Miracles"—Miyoshi Umeki
"I Enjoy Being a Girl"—Pat Suzuki
"I Am Going to Like It Here"—Miyoshi Umeki
"Like a God"—Ed Kenney
"Chop Suey"—Juanita Hall, Patrick Adiarte, ensemble
"Don't Marry Me"—Larry Blyden, Miyoshi Umeki
"Grant Avenue"—Pat Suzuki, ensemble
"Love, Look Away"—Arabella Hong
"Fan Tan Fannie"—Anita Ellis
"Gliding Through My Memoree"—Jack Soo, girls
"The Other Generation"—Juanita Hall, Kaye Luke
"Sunday"—Pat Suzuki, Larry Blyden
NOTE: "My Best Love" dropped before opening.

1959. THE SOUND OF MUSIC
       Producer: Leland Hayward, Richard Halliday, Rodgers and
          Hammerstein
       Libretto: Howard Lindsay and Russel Crouse
       Director: Vincent J. Donehue
       Musical numbers: Joe Layton
       New York Run: November 16, 1959–
       "Preludium"–Nuns
       "The Sound of Music"–Mary Martin
       "Maria"–Patricia Neway, Muriel O'Malley, Elizabeth
          Howell, Karen Shepard
       "My Favorite Things"–Mary Martin, Patricia Neway
       "Do Re Mi"–Mary Martin, children
       "Sixteen Going On Seventeen"–Brian Davies, Lauri Peters
       "The Lonely Goatherd"–Mary Martin, children
       "How Can Love Survive?"–Marion Marlowe, Kurt
          Kasznar, Theodore Bikel
       "So Long, Farewell"–Children
       "Climb Ev'ry Mountain"–Patricia Neway
       "No Way to Stop It"–Theodore Bikel, Kurt Kasznar,
          Marion Marlowe
       "An Ordinary Couple"–Mary Martin, Theodore Bikel
       "Edelweiss"–Theodore Bikel

Index

[183